The Matchbook Advertising Company

ADNAN SERIFOGLU

THE MATCHBOOK ADVERTISING COMPANY
GOOD AND BAD EMPLOYEE MANAGEMENT

2009

The Matchbook Advertising Company

TABLE OF CONTENTS

PREFACE AND ACKNOWLEDGEMENTS

B anks and financial institutions can only be partly held responsible for the current recession and there are many other reasons that eventually led to unexpected failures of sound and established businesses and even to that of prime banks and financing houses.

A factor that could have caused most untimely business failures may have resulted from aggressive and almost obsessive marketing initiatives that created unsustainable levels of demand. This attitude indeed has a relation to the level of employee commitment and content from the CEO level down, particularly during critical phases of company operations.

This is a readable book that looks at how people could be best fit in an organizational context as well as at the needs of the human asset. Although there are no easy solutions to highly complex people-related issues, this book may provide an analytic appraisal for the seasoned manager.

Wherever possible, I acknowledged the sources of the knowledge contained in this book and my grateful thanks and gratitude are for Peter Drucker, Douglas McGregor, Dale Yoder, Frederick Herzberg, to name only a few of the remarkable people who are in the public domain and without whose research and contributions, this book could never have been possible.

PART I
THE BASICS

CHAPTER 1
Systems

Anything that works, regardless whether it is a living organism or a machine must have an organized system in which all the parts run uniformly to form a whole. A company is not any different, regardless whether it is a bakery employing only ten people or is an international corporate empire employing thousands of people. Two basic elements are needed for this organizational structure to function:

- The employer, or organization
- The public responsibility, or laws and regulations

THE EMPLOYER

Obviously the employer is the most critical element. It is the employer that takes on all the risks, invests all needed capital, prepares the working conditions, hires the manpower, trains employees through various types of on-the-job training, compensates employees, assigns jobs, arranges work shifts and employee job transfers, rewards deserving employees with promotion to higher-paying jobs, coordinates the functioning of various services relating to employee welfare and their needs, ensures that safety and health standards are maintained and has overall responsibility for successful management of the enterprise.

In addition, the employer must make sure the company turns a profit as well.

An employer also needs to ensure that the company has got

all its 'hygiene' factors in place. The Oxford Dictionary quotes hygiene as "cleanliness as a means of preventing disease".

In our context this means, "Make sure that your house is in order".

LAWS AND THE PUBLIC RESPONSIBILITY

Today's industrial environment is controlled by legislation. With the declared aim that this is needed for the protection of the public interest, the influence of labour legislation is quite clearly felt through the various government agencies that exert these controls over workplace activities. Here are some of the areas within the scope of these agencies:

- Conditions for the employment of women and children.
- Minimum payable wages and maximum work hours.
- Inspecting work conditions for safety and health needs.
- Ensuring that employees are insured against worksite accidents and that premiums are paid into funds for government-operated medical and retirement systems.
- Overseeing employer-union relations to ensure that the legal requirements are met and to generally maintain the industrial peace.
- Aiding in keeping records of job vacancy availability and helping in job placements, as well as operating public vocational job training programs.

There are other responsibilities as well. The scope and extent of application of these industrial laws may differ from one country to the other.

In almost all countries in the world today, these laws now also include provisions that allow the activity of labour unions on behalf of company employees. This has naturally brought about the need to now include labour or trade unions as the third element in modern industrial life.

THE UNION

Historically, labour or trade unions came about to help provide better working conditions and terms of employment and to enhance the welfare levels of industrial workers. Union activity heightened over the years that followed the 'industrial revolution' to deal with unjust arbitrary actions of ruthless employers depicted by novelists such as Charles Dickens and others. Modern Unions since then have over the years evolved into becoming a significant force in industrial life. The basic areas of labour or trade union responsibilities are:

- To negotiate on behalf of all union-member employees for collective work agreements, mainly to determine rates of wages, hours of work as well as many other conditions of employment.
- To monitor that the conditions contained in the collective agreements are not violated at the worksite, through union-representative employees who have been appointed by the union as authorised 'shop stewards'. There are many other union responsibilities as well. The scope and extent of application of these laws relating to union activity can differ from one country to the other. Union activity may cover some of the following:

STRIKE AND LOCKOUTS

Depending on the terms of the laws that cover collective negotiations, should a dispute arise over an agreement between the employer and the union, the union is eligible to call for a total stop in production at the employer's workplace and to direct its members to go on 'strike', or to stop work. Since this step is a legal one, employers may not take any disciplinary action against these employees beyond stopping all wage payments.

On the other hand, the employer too can take similar legal action and declare what is termed as a 'lockout', which is stopping any company employee from entering the worksite.

UNION MEMBERSHIP AND COLLECTIVE BARGAINING

Many companies have a cut-off line whereby its supervisors and managers are considered to be outside the scope of union membership. In general, companies may not legally refuse union membership to its employees.

Depending on the terms of the laws, unions would become eligible to negotiate with a company when more than one half of the number of company employees join that union. The company management then needs to decide on some of the following issues:

Where to negotiate?
- Within company premises?
- Outside site?
- Alternate between union premises and company office?

Who should negotiate?
- Although lawyers could assist in providing legal advice, the tendency to delegate union negotiations to lawyers is not much favored by both management and unions. The reason for this is that they can be too legalistic in their approach and could slow down

negotiations because of lack of knowledge of the actual working conditions.
- Line managers of the individual employers should form part of a company negotiating team.
- There is some support for union negotiations to be conducted by an association of several companies within the same industry sector; however the use of 'outside' negotiators could have benefits as well as disadvantages, and needs to be weighed.

Negotiate on company time?
- Practice varies on who pays for negotiating time spent by company employee union representatives. The standard is paid leave of absence for actual negotiating sessions but no overtime paid in the event the sessions exceed usual working hours.

Negotiating rules and procedure?
- Make sure that the union is authorized to conduct negotiation on behalf of the employees
- Begin with a presentation or exchange of proposals.
- Be friendly and introduce everybody. Relieve any tensions.
- Have a committee of employees available to give advice, if needed.
- Listen to the other side. Give everybody the chance to state own positions. Respect, courtesy and common sense must prevail.
- Don't set deadlines or rush negotiators. Although an agreement could very possibly ensue because of this deadline, the resulting agreement may not be what both parties can live with.
- Arbitration should only be used as a last resort.

What are Management Prerogatives?

Management needs to freely exercise actions that relate to the conduct of its own business without any outside interference, provided that it does not violate the terms of collective employment agreements that it has concluded with the union. Some of these rights are:

- Right to determine policy on finance, interest rates, loans, etc
- Right to determine sales policies, organization, market area, export sales.
- Right to select the materials, processes and the products to be manufactured
- Right to select location and structure of company plants
- Right to select the machine tools and the production locations
- Right to determine company production schedules and basically
- The right to freely hire and dismiss its employees, to train, to transfer, to promote, to discipline, to grant leave of absences, to grant merit increases, to determine salary scales and employee job grades.

Protect your Management Prerogatives:

Management prerogatives are important for companies to enable them to conduct their business effectively. Make sure that

- Management Prerogatives are safeguarded.
- The union does legally represent the majority of your workforce.
- You are clear about the jobs that are exempt from union membership.
- Your policy is fair and ethical treatment of all employees, regardless of any union membership status.

CHAPTER 2
The Matchbook Advertising Company

Ever since I can remember, companies that had become smaller by shedding some of their manpower were considered to have become more efficient and robust. Staff dismissals had been necessary for modernizing the operation or for reducing inventory, in which case this downsizing had been for a good cause and was a fine thing. The only problem was that the employee dismissals and layoffs had not been very pleasant, but so be it.

The other day I happened to come across someone talking on TV about how easy it is to start up a business. I turned up the volume out of curiosity.

"Enterprises come about whenever the needed three factors are present", he was saying, "Land, capital in the form of machinery or plant and the needed human resources, which is the employees".

It occurred to me at that moment that I had really never come across any other resource, such as the machinery or plant equipment or even raw materials being disposed of during any of these cost cuttings exercises. Simply reducing that most expensive variable asset, which is the human resource had made all the difference and put the company back on track.

Why it has ever been necessary to call normal people human resource is really beyond me.

In May 1972, I was forced to dismiss five hard-working young men and ladies when I liquidated a promising company I had started about a year ago.

The look of surprise on the faces of some, of hurt feelings and that of bravado on yet the others are expressions that I am not ever likely to forget.

I had set up this company for a venture that appeared to have nowhere to go but up and to succeed tremendously. An industrial boom had just started up and there were yet no modern advertising agencies to meet these pressing needs. The company shareholders and I had decided that producing advertising giveaways was a most attractive business so our company had been formed to manufacture matchbooks for advertising purposes.

We found just the right size compact matchbook-producing machine manufactured by a company in Japan and were now discussing the order.

Our company was registered in May 1971 and titled The Matchbook Advertising Company, Limited.

We had in the meantime logged several orders for advertisement matchbooks with the top hotels and restaurants in Ankara and in Istanbul with the expectation that our machine would be delivered within a few months.

Our first serious setback was when the bank turned down our import credit application and we had no luck with any of the other banks.

We had booked several orders that needed to be filled. I managed to reach an agreement with the only matchbook manufacturer in Istanbul to produce these on our behalf and we managed to fill these orders at almost no profit. The shareholders and I decided to diversify into other advertising give-away products and started to produce beer-mats and key-chains and several other similar products.

Our pre-tax profit for the first year was 56%, with a projection of 32% for the next year, calculated by our chartered accountant.

At the beginning of the second year however, our company started to experience severe liquidity problems and difficulties in payroll payments.

I went to the office of the chartered accountant and examined all the company records and books. Here is what we found.

1. Only partial payments had been made for three major orders. Raising the invoice and collecting payment are two different actions.

2. We had no idea of the extent of our salary overpayments. Even my salary as the company manager was excessively high.

3. There was no possibility that we would ever reach the projected profit target for the coming year.

It is certainly easy to start up a company anywhere you like and in any part of the world, provided that there are laws regulating formation of commercial enterprises. The success of any business venture however is mainly dependent on two major factors:

1. Contented and productive employees

2. "Fair" wages and salaries that are carefully monitored

3. Effective cost controls

There is nothing novel in any of this. All the merchants, traders or bankers, notably the Medici banking enterprise of the 14th century employed well-paid staff, judging from their highly successful transactions in the foreign countries of the time.

Good employee management is not easy to explain, because it is neither a benevolent attitude nor is it any form of disciplined employment practice. In fact it is the exact opposite of a carrots and whip management approach.

When Germany was severely defeated at the end of the Second World War, the Soviets and the Allies had razed most of its industries to rabble. The dispirited and wounded combatants, who could, returned to their homes and families with little hope of surviving into the future. Prosperity, peace and contentment seemed to be an impossible dream.

Although it is undocumented, there are several accounts of German industrialists who came to some form of understanding with previous craftsmen employees that had survived the horrors of the war. Loyalty to the company was the main factor in a voluntary agreement that no salary would be paid nor claimed for periods that could extend to over 1 or even 2 years during the reconstruction phase.

There are reports that these industrialists, notably the Krupp industries of Essen, arranged for some form of black market supplies of food essentials to the workers and to their families during these difficult times.

The Japanese industrial reconstruction is almost parallel in likeness to that of the German example.

Breakthroughs and spectacular successes in the US have always come through ingenious and sometimes lucky, teamwork projects. The common quality of employees in all the three examples had been devotion to the company that was totally based on contentment.

What is the point then of having happy and contented employees if the company is not profitable? Yet, there is an uncanny connection between contented employees and company profits.

This book looks into this phenomenon and suggests ways and means of how this can actually be worked and perhaps achieved.

The first part of the book outlines brief basics.

The second part is a scenario outline on some simple steps for establishing the business venture, which in our case is called the SOFI Corporation.

The third part describes some simple and useful tools for good employee management and that of the final part returns to the SOFI Corporation scenario with outlines of various options available to the SOFI Corporation business venture.

Leading companies rightfully place great importance on the good company image and always have time and effort to ensure that it is enhanced.

The balance sheets in most of their annual reports sometimes fluctuate in profits from year to year but one basic element always comes through in these company reports; the invariable statement of how proud the company is of its people asset and of its employees who have over the years carried the company to its present position.

This good image did not come about through meticulous planning by people nor did good advertising strategy or successful public relations much to do with it.

The Japanese industrial companies continually compete with each other in promoting their company as the best opportunity for the right person. Many top class corporations in the US and in Europe also advertise in this vein, targeting the average person with the message that their company is a good place to work for and assures a successful career for the right person.

Good company image come from all walks of life and it is not just the opinion of industry leaders, statesmen or top professionals. The average person must also think highly of the company and it is important that farmers, plumbers, taxi drivers or bartenders say, "That's a great company" whenever the company name is mentioned.

The CEOs and top managers of these companies deserve a "hats off to you" compliment and to feel that special glow and tingle of being right in the satisfaction of knowing that trust and delegation has handsomely paid off in profits.

CHAPTER 3
Jobs

A job means any number of positions performing <u>APPROXIMATELY</u> the same task. Just one person can only fill any position, whereas several people doing the same work can occupy the same job.

A job can be that of ambulance drivers employed by large complex hospitals or it could be that of an ambulance driver working for a private company with its own medical center.

A job can sometimes be a similar job performed by all the workers in the company.

The job description outlines what the job is all about. For example, it is necessary to use a job description in order to pay the right wage for the right job in your company and to base this on the price of the job in the marketplace.

The job that your worker performs in your company could be EASIER or MORE DIFFICULT to perform than that of the marketplace. A job description is therefore needed to make the right comparison between these jobs.

A job description also explains to your employees exactly what is expected from them and can improve morale by outlining the importance of their jobs. It is essentially a list of what to do.

Because the job description is basically a list of tasks, this can also be used inform the recruiters what the job is all about and what sort of person they need to look for in filling the job.

Some of the uses of job descriptions are:

- To explain in a step-by-step format exactly what is expected from your employees

- To inform recruiters what this job is about and what sort of person to look for

- To allow the work to be analyzed in a step-by-step format so that if needed, the job can be simplified and changed so it can be performed by lesser-skilled workers at lower cost

- To identify the kind of training needed to perform the job so that this can be a guide in developing training programs

- Allow for easy "pricing" of the job based on the community market rates to pay "fair" wages

- Allow the "ranking" of all jobs in the company and to pay employees according to the responsibility and weight of the jobs

- Understand the safety hazards of the job as described in the job description and use this as a guide in developing a work safety program

Job descriptions have many other uses for a company.

Who should prepare job descriptions?

In some cases, employees themselves have been asked to write out their own job descriptions, because they would best know the most important elements of the job. The common practice today however is to have professional job analysts interview the jobholder and to prepare standard format descriptions.

One reason for this approach is that "timing" of the jobs could be necessary, especially when manufacturing plants are being set up for the first time. A stopwatch is most commonly used to measure repetitive manufacturing tasks. Should, for example a job consist of 4 separate and simple repetitive acts that are:

1. Take up two identical metal pieces from tray
2. Insert a rivet in the holes holding both pieces together
3. Machine stamp the rivet into the hole
4. Place this assembly in the moving tray on the production belt

The time that each of these acts takes must be carefully measured as accurately as possible over as many samplings to determine the optimum average job time.

Another reason for a standardizing the job description format throughout the company is to enable its use in analyzing jobs prior to classifying, or rating the jobs in a ranking exercise for the whole company.

CHAPTER 4
Rating or Classification of Jobs

1) JOB RATINGS ARE NEEDED TO PAY THE RIGHT WAGE FOR THE RIGHT JOB:

Job classification is also called JOB RATING or JOB GRADING. This is a management tool that is essential to pay the right price for the right job.

Job ratings are mostly used to "fit" in the right caliber of manpower when selecting staff and to pay attractive market-rate salaries.

For example, if our business were a pastry shop that we know from experience will need about 10 people to operate, our next step is obviously to pay the same wages to the employees doing the same work.

Suppose our pastry shop needs exactly ten people in five different jobs: One shop manager, two bakers, 4 shop helpers, 1 cashier and 2 baker helpers.

The pastry shop owner's first step would be to actually visit as many other pastry shops in the area to find out exactly what they were paying their employees.

To do this properly, the pastry shop proprietor needs to first prepare simple job descriptions of the work that the employees are expected to do so that a comparison of the various jobs can be made.

All our jobs turn out to be almost identical with those of the other pastry shops, with the exception of the shop helpers, the cashier and the shop manager, who are also expected to understand and speak some French. The reason for this is because the new pastry shop would most probably cater to the many French companies operating in the district, as well as to the staff of the nearby French Embassy.

The pastry shop owner found that the market pay rates for these 5 jobs were:

***

Job Group 5, Shop Mgr, Market Minimum $1760, Mid $1955, Max $2150

Job Group 4, Baker, Market Minimum $1430, Mid $1590, Max $1750

Job Group 3, Cashier, Market Minimum $1160, Mid $1290, Max $1420

Job Group 2, Shop Help, Market Minimum $940, Mid $1045, Max $1150

Job Group 1, Cleaner/Help, Market Minimum $760, Mid $845, Max $930

An example of a simple-format job description used by the pastry shop:

***

JOB DESCRIPTION -Job Group and Title: JG 1-Baker Helper/cleaner

Scope of Work

The Pastry Shop is located in the city's major business area and close to the French Embassy.

The Baker Helper/Cleaner works six days a week 9.00-21.00 with one-hour lunch break. The whole pastry shop

THE MATCHBOOK ADVERTISING COMPANY

and bakery areas must be clean and sanitary at all times
to reflect the image of a quality pastry shop

Scope of Coverage
The Baker Helper/cleaners work on a 12-hour work
schedule with a one-hour lunch break and one rest day off
taken in turn with teammate.

Description of duties:
The cleaner is one of 2 people who follow a preset plan for
vacuuming and mop cleaning of all shop areas including the
bakery and storage. areas. Work involves emptying waste
bins, sweeping and mopping floor surfaces, cleaning all
toilets and other areas as assigned. The cleaners also notify
any appliances needing repair or replacement to the Bakers,
to whom they report. They operate dough machinery and
monitor ovens and other tasks as set out by the Bakers. They
are required to maintain polite and good communication
with all colleagues or customers at all times.

Mental/Education requirement:
Incumbents need to have primary school education with
good knowledge of the basics of hygienic and sanitary
conditions.

Skill/Experience required:
Basically, no experience is needed but they must display
basic politeness in human relations and need to undergo
2-day orientation training, including fire prevention and
safety, as they may be required to react immediately in
emergency.

<u>Physical Effort needed:</u>	60% standing and 40% moving about.
<u>Responsibilities/Impact on results:</u>	<u>Minimal.</u>
<u>Working Conditions/Safety</u>	The shop is in the city business area.
<u>Points (x Factor in $)</u>	$760 - $845 - $930 (x1)

2) JOB RATINGS ARE NEEDED TO KNOW WHAT CALIBRE OF PERSON TO HIRE:

Using job descriptions that now also have a "price" and a grading, the pastry shop owner is able to advertise for the jobs and to explain exact job requirements.

In fact, the pastry shop owner can now decide on what to pay for each person in the job on the basis of differences in:

- Age
- Experience
- Skills
- Educational background
- Other qualities such as languages, other.

This is what the pastry shop owner finally ended up with:

JG 5, Shop Mgr, Salary $2400, Min $1760, Mid $1955, Max $ 2150

JG 4, Baker1, Salary$2000, Min $ 1430,Mid $ 1590, Max $ 1750

JG 4, Baker2, Salary$1750, Min $ 1430,Mid $ 1590, Max $ 1750

JG 3, Cashier, Salary $1160, Min $1160, Mid $1290, Max $1420

JG 2, Shop Help1,2,3, Salary $800, Min $940, Mid $1045, Max $1150

JG 2, Shop Help4, Salary $1000, Min $940, Mid $1045, Max $1150

JG 1, Cleaner/Help1, Salary $700, Min $760, Mid $845, Max $930

JG 1, Cleaner/Help2, Salary $760, Min $760, Mid $845, Max $930

It seems that the pastry shop proprietor had difficulty in finding an experienced manager with good knowledge of French and needed to pay $250 more than the maximum salary in the community.

Hiring the top quality bakers also posed a problem; all the good ones were already working for competitor pastry shops. The pastry shop proprietor had to offer higher salaries to entice the bakers to move to the new job.

Hiring the shop helpers was not at all difficult and three young newcomers were hired at lower salaries for the new pastry shop.

An outline of how the advertisements actually took place and how the candidates were interviewed and finally selected will be outlined in a following chapter related to the recruitment process.

3) CLASSIFICATION OF JOBS ARE NEEDED FOR JOB TRANSFERS OR PROMOTIONS

It is important in determining the needs of the jobs

in the event of transfers or promotions and to pay the right compensation for promoted staff.

4) GRADES

The grades for each job on the market will allow the company to adapt these market minimums and maximum rates to its own salary administration system.

The company can then use these market rates with some minor adjustments to reflect the actual needs of each job in the company.

5) MARKET MINIMUM AND MAXIMUM RATES

Basically in principle, employers should avoid paying less than the minimum for each job on the market. Similarly the company should not, unless there are exceptional reasons, pay more than the current maximum salary for that job in the marketplace.

6) MONITORING EMPLOYEE SALARY PROGRESSIONS

The progress of each employee within these salary ranges needs to be closely monitored to determine approximately where the employee is in percentage terms within the range. This management tool is called "COMPA-RATIO" and is of particular importance in keeping a "finger on the pulse" on manpower costs as well as for good budgetary controls.

There are simply too many cases of successful companies

that have folded just because they had imagined their manpower costs were under control.

The Compa-ratio will be outlined in detail in chapter 9.

PART II
THE SOFI CORPORATION SCENARIO

CHAPTER 5
Establishing the Company

Assume that you work for a well-known European manufacturer of small household appliances. The corporate headquarters is located in Geneva and you have headed the company's North African division for the past 4 years. The market share in your territory has considerably improved over the years and is regularly rising. Your recent performance discussion has focused on the positive aspects of your pleasant personality and natural ability to get along with people from many different cultural backgrounds. This has obviously helped you to attain this level of success.

Your staff are supportive and loyal and company employees of all levels at the headquarter complex seem to like you.

You have recently been offered a new position to head a unique joint venture involving the formal establishment of a totally new manufacturing company, SOFI Corporation, in a country of your selection, for approval of the board. You and your wife have discussed this opportunity and decided to accept this challenging appointment.

It is planned that the new plant will be setup to manufacture and export household appliances directly to the emerging markets in several countries surrounding the Black Sea and Caspian regions. These products are presently being exported directly from the company's plant at Munich.

The new company has been formed in a partnership with a group of South Asian financiers entailing a 10-year low-interest bank loan investment of US$80 million for this venture. The expected annual net return on the investment is between 15%-16%.

You had extensively traveled over the past two months and researched many investment possibilities in North African, Mediterranean and East European countries.

The board has now approved your recommendation to establish the manufacturing plant at a suitable location in one of Turkey's industrial belt areas located not too far from Istanbul. Legal counsel have supported and helped you in processing all the needed applications and registrations and the new company has now been formally established.

The Plant:

You have concluded a 10-year renewable lease for a suitable factory complex that had previously been used as a washing machine assembly plant. The manufacturer has moved to a larger integrated complex in the Thrace region.

You consider yourself to be fortunate that semi-skilled labor is readily available in the region and that there are several other industrial plants in the area. The complex you have leased is ideal in that there is one main factory building of the right size to accommodate your planned production lines. The management building is a quaint two-story building with a large dining hall and kitchen facilities on the ground floor.

The warehouse storage building and ancillaries are exceptionally well suited to your needs. The whole complex is well protected. A high perimeter fence that is well illuminated provides good security during the night. There are also several other smaller buildings, one of which could be used as an emergency medical center.

There are now several other steps that you will need to take. You have been given a brief to manufacture the following for a predetermined product sales volume to subsidiaries in several countries in the Black Sea and Caspian regions:

***

	DAILY	MONTHLY	YEARLY	SALES
HOUSEHOLD IRONS	2000	60000	660,000	$11,880,000
COOLER-HEATER	1000	30000	330,000	$29,040,000
WATER FOUNTAIN				
HAIR CONDITIONER	2000	60000	660,000	$5,280,000
			TOTAL	$46,200,000

Your basic first step has been to hire a Personnel Management Director with the right plant management experience in a similar industry environment. It was also necessary to hire a qualified and experienced bi-lingual Executive Secretary to assist yourself and the Personnel Management Director during the critical start-up phase. The company head office has arranged with the Munich plant to support you with a team of 3 specialists, who will conduct the necessary time and motion studies. The total fastest average times required for each repetitive production action has determined that the needed production could be met by semi-skilled labor working on two 8-hour shifts with a 30-minute meal break. The management rationale for starting off with two shifts was based on a contingency plan in the case production is required to be scaled down; in this event there will be only one shift.

Initially, on each of the two 8-hour shifts, there would be

- 4 belts requiring 10 shift workers each to assemble 1000 irons/shift
- 2 belts with 8 shift workers each to assemble 500 water fountains per shift

- 8 belts with 10 shift workers each to assemble 1000 hair conditioners per shift

The need to cover for weekly rest days, illnesses and other worker absenteeism necessitates that a total of 56 regular + 16 relief =72 shift workers are hired:

Hereunder is an example of a simple 1-page job description for the typical shift worker:

***

JOB DESCRIPTION- Job Group and Title: JG 1- Shift Worker

Scope of Work
On each 2 8-hour shifts, there are
- 4 belts with 10 shift workers each for 2000 irons per day
- 2 belts with 8 shift workers each for 1000 water fountains per day
- 8 belts with 10 shift workers each for 2000 hair conditioners per day

Scope of the Shift Worker Coverage
Incumbent is a shift worker on prod belt with one rest day on any day of the week with 11 months work and month of July as paid holiday

Description of duties:
Shift Worker is one of 8-10 workers who perform basically **REPETITIVE** and **BORING** work for the safe and uninterrupted production of household appliances. The production belt will suspend activity for 30- minutes in mid shifts to allow for a meal break as coordinated and monitored by the shift Foreman.

<u>Mental/Education requirement</u>:
Must be able to change wiring in any simple electric wall plug. Minimum primary school graduate with some knowledge of technical basics.

<u>Skill/Experience required</u>:No previous experience required. Must display basic politeness in human relations and should undergo 2-week basic factory training, including safety. Danger of the work requires immediate preventive reaction for protection to factory and to self.

<u>Physical Effort needed</u>:
85% standing and 15% moving about. Must be able and robust.

<u>Responsibilities/Impact on results:</u>
Could be partly responsible for $45000 worth of product during each shift and could be eventually responsible for worst-case production loss of $630000 per week.

<u>Working Conditions/Safety</u>
High noise, rapidly moving machine parts and presence of safety hazards

<u>Points (Factor x)</u>   545 – 605- 665 (x1)

We have now ascertained the approximate total manning required for the factory shift worker's job.

Our next step was to prepare simple 1-page-format job descriptions for all jobs in SOFI Corporation so that we know what sort of staff we will need to recruit and hire.

Ascertaining numbers at this stage is at best a calculable educated guess, based on comparisons of the number of people required in similar capacity operations.

Essentially extrapolating from the number of shift workers in the manufacturing operation, our manpower figures have worked out as hereunder:

***

MANNING REQUIREMENT FOR SOFI A.S.

Factory production (2x8 hour shifts)	Shift Worker	Shift Quality Control	Shift Quality Control Eng	Packing/Shipping Assistants	Safety Eng	Prod Manager	Total
	72	16	8	20	4	2	122
Factory Support (3x8 hour shifts)	Maintenance Mechanic	Electrician	Warehouse Asst	Forklift Operator	Security	Cleaners	Total
	6	2	2	2	7	6	25
Normal Operations- (9 hours x5day week)	Receptionist/ Operator	Cooks	Secretaries	Accts Staff	Sales Staff	Services Staff	Total
	2	2	3	4	4	3	18
Normal Operations- Management (9 hours x5day week)	Marketing Manager	Finance Manager	Personnel Management Director	Legal/PR Manager	Plant Manager	General Manager	Total
	1	1	1	1	1	1	6
Medical Support	Doctor	Nurse & Ambulance Driver					Total
	1	3					4
Training Staff	2						2
TOTAL				177			

All of the Sofi Corporation job descriptions were prepared in a simple format and not more than 1 page long.

This now allows us to visit the other factories in the area and try to identify what we need to pay each grade of our employees.

There are a total of 27 jobs in our company. The General Manager's job description is given hereunder as an example:

***

THE MATCHBOOK ADVERTISING COMPANY

JOB DESCRIPTION-Job Group/title: General Manager, JG 13

Scope of Work
The main office and warehouse -shipping works a normal workweek from Monday-Friday between
9.00-   18.00 with a one-hour lunch. The production plant operates 11 months in the year on 2x8hour shifts.

Scope of Work Coverage
SOFI Corporation produces unique electrical household appliances and is located in Bozüyük (Turkey). The General Manager has overall manufacturing and marketing responsibility for this fully integrated company employing nearly 200 direct company employees and contractors providing different services.

Description of duties:
The General Manager of the company is mainly responsible for profitability and stock value of the company through accurate strategic planning. The General Manager reports directly to the board of directors at the group main office in Geneva and is ultimately responsible for profitability and management of the plant. Executive action takes place by delegation to the department managers.

Mental and education requirement:
A degree in an engineering discipline is desirable; an MBA degree is a plus.

Skill/Experience required:
A minimum of 10-year experience is required at an international position in a similar industry. Fluency in English (and one other European or Asian language) is essential. He needs to possess a high level of intellectual maturity to properly manage this challenging job.

Physical Effort needed:
10% standing, 30% moving about and 60% sitting.

Responsibilities/Impact on results:
The General Manager is not only responsible for his own actions but also for that of others in the company. He is vested with full responsibility in all executive action and financial action, either directly or by others in the company. Most of his activity is interaction with employees and major clients. The overall value of the company shares on the stock market is directly related to his industrial actions.

Working Conditions/Safety
The office is located about 6 kilometers from the center of the town.

Points (x Factor)
6550-   7300 – 8040 (x 1.9)

All the **SOFI CORPORATION** job descriptions are included as a reference at the end of this book..

The focus in these job descriptions is on the simplicity and ease of reading them. This is necessary if we want total strangers to look at our job descriptions and whose only possible reason to help us is fully out of basic courtesy and based upon our promise that we will certainly do likewise to help them whenever needed in future.

We need to compare apples with apples and oranges with oranges and make sure that the jobs of both factories are really the same. Our task is not easy; for example most of the secretary jobs in the other companies were required to be bi-lingual in at least one foreign language with a minimum of 5 years experience. Our Secretary jobs are much lighter in terms of qualification and only the Executive Secretary's job, which is in a higher job group, needed to be bi-lingual.

Therefore most of our jobs turned out to be either *more difficult* or *easier.* Our Project Team was able to devise a workable formula that states the difficulty levels in easily understandable percentage terms.

For example, the forklift operator's job in the community is simple operation of the forklift with no need to make any complicated spacing calculations or apply any of the logistic decisions made by our warehouse staff. Our forklift operator is calculated to be 20% more complicated and difficult to perform compared with the average community job. The SOFI Corp forklift operator's salary may therefore be 20% higher compared to that of the community average pay for forklift operators.

CHAPTER 6
Wage & Salary Administration

All companies need to have their own wage & salary administration system (generally called salary structure or range) so that they are able to pay equitable salaries and to attract and keep the services of desired people in the company.

This is vital from the point of cost control and accurate manpower budgeting. Especially important in the industrial scene of today is the need to maintain projections for the eventuality of union collective bargaining and vital financial salary controls.

All companies pay "fringe benefits" in some form or the other. They are called by various names, such as bonuses, premium payment, overtime differential payments, meal and clothing allowances, shift differentials, holiday incentives, medical incentives, etc.

Company salary ranges is basic pay only and DOES NOT contain any fringe benefits. Salary ranges are also needed to reward deserving employees if and when they are given a good performance rating and to form a criterion for promotions or location transfers.

Based on the community survey, we have been able to grade and classify all our jobs into 13 categories, called job groups, with the top General Manager's in the highest grade, job group 13 and the lowest-graded job, those of the semi-skilled Shift Workers and the Cleaners in job group 1.

Our discussions with the 7 factories that participated in our salary survey revealed that the jobs of the semi-skilled shift workers are almost identical. The general test of skill levels were simple tasks such as ability to change the wiring in an electric wall plug and/or similar. We also ascertained that suitable semi-skilled manpower is readily available and live within a radius of 7-10 kilometers. As practiced by the other factories, we will also use a fleet of leased minibuses to transport the shift workforce to and from the factory.

We have also ascertained that the community practice is that meals are served in all the other factories to the shift workforce and that it would be more feasible to operate our own kitchen facilities compared to outsourced catering. We have budgeted for suitable cooks and the kitchen staff.

***

Community Market Survey Results ($per month)
JG 13, Gen Mgr, 1, Min $6550, Mid $7300, Max $6040
JG 12, Plant Mgr, 1, Min $5330, Mid $5935, Max $6535
JG 11, Marketing Mgr, 1, Min $4330, Mid $4825, Max $5320
JG 11, Prod Mgr, 2, Min $4330, Mid $4825, Max $5320
JG 10, Personnel Director, 1, Min $3580, Mid $4000, Max $4370
JG 10, Legal/PR Mgr, 1, Min $3580, Mid $4000, Max $4370
JG 10, Finance Mgr, 1, Min $3580, Mid $4000, Max $4370
JG9, Safety Engineer, 4, Min $2865, Mid $3180, Max $3500
JG9, Quality Cont Eng, 8, Min $2865, Mid $3180, Max $3500

JG9, Doctor, 1, Min $2865, Mid $3180, Max $3500

JG8, Exec Secretary, 1, Min $2365, Mid $2630, Max $2890

JG8, Sales Staff, 4, Min $2365, Mid $2630, Max $2890

JG8, Training Staff, 2, Min $2365, Mid $2630, Max $2890

JG7, Secretary, 3, Min $1900, $2110, $2320

JG6, Pack/Ship Asst, 20, Min $1545, Mid $1720, Max $1890

JG6, Accounts Staff, 4, Min $1545, Mid $1720, Max $1890

JG6, Services Staff, 3, Min $1545, Mid $1720, Max $1890

JG6, Receptionist/Oprt, 2, Min $1545, Mid $1720, Max $1890

JG5, Maint Mechanic, 6, Min $1260, Mid $1400, Max $1540

JG5, Electrician, 2, Min $1260, Mid $1400, Max $1540

JG5, Warehouse Asst, 2, Min $1260, Mid $1400, Max $1540

JG4, Forklift Oprt, 2, Min $1020, Mid $1135, Max $1245

JG4, Quality Cont F/man, 16, Min $1020, Mid $1135, Max $1245

JG4, Forklift Oprt, 2, Min $1020, Mid $1135, Max $1245

JG4, Nurse/Driver, 3, Min $1020, Mid $1135, Max $1245

JG 3, Security Guard, 7, Min $830, Mid $920, Max $1015

JG 2, Cook, 2, Min $675, Mid $750, Max $825

JG 1, Shift Worker, 72, Min $545, Mid $605, Max $665

JG 1, Cleaner, 6, Min $545, Mid $605, Max $665

Total Employees 177

Our research has revealed that the following SOFI

Corporation jobs are *heavier,* or *lighter,* than those in the community market:

1. General Manager: 90% *heavier*
2. Plant Manager: 60% *heavier*
3. Production Manager: 30% *heavier*
4. Marketing Manager: 30% *heavier*
5. Finance Manager: 10% *lighter*
6. Legal and PR Manager: 10% *lighter*
7. Personnel Mgmt Direct.: 10% *lighter*
8. Safety Engineer: 10% *heavier*
9. Shift Quality Eng: 10% *heavier*
10. Training Staff : 20% *heavier*
11. Sales Staff : 20% *heavier*
12. Executive Secretary: 20% *heavier*
13. Secretary: 10% *lighter*
14. Services Assistant: 20% *heavier*
15. Packing/Shipping Asst: 20% *heavier*
16. Receptionist: 20% *heavier*
17. Accounts Asst: 20% *heavier*
18. Maintenance Mechanic: 20% *heavier*
19. Electrician: 20% *heavier*
20. Warehouse Asst: 20% *heavier*
21. Forklift Operator: 20% *heavier*
22. Shift Quality Control: 20% *heavier*
23. Nurse/Ambulance Driver: 20% *heavier*

Depending on the job minimums being lighter or heavier than the market rate, SOFI Corporation monthly base salaries are as shown hereunder.

While the employees in most of the jobs were paid the market minimum, others in jobs that are scarce in the market were hired at the market average or at an even higher starting salary, depending on age or experience. Heavier is shown as (+%) and lighter is (-%).

***

Sofi Corporation Salaries and Ranges ($per month)

JG 13, Gen Mgr, 1, Salary $12445, Min $6550, Mid $7300, Max $6040 (+90%)

JG 12, Plant Mgr, 1, Salary $8530, Min $5330, Mid $5935, Max $6535 (+60%)

JG 11, Marketing Mgr, 1, Salary $5630, Min $4330, Mid $4825, Max $5320 (+30%)

JG 11, Prod Mgr, 2, Salary $5630, Min $4330, Mid $4825, Max $5320 (+30%)

JG 10, Personnel Director, 1, Salary $3560, Min $3580, Mid $4000, Max $4370(-10%)

JG 10, Legal/PR Mgr, 1, Salary $3560, Min $3580, Mid $4000, Max $4370 (-10%)

JG 10, Finance Mgr, 1, Salary $3560, Min $3580, Mid $4000, Max $4370 (-10%)

JG9, Safety Engineer, 4, Salary $3150, Min $2865, Mid $3180, Max $3500 (+10%)

JG9, Quality Cont Eng, 8, Salary $3150, Min $2865, Mid $3180, Max $3500 (+10%)

JG9, Doctor, 1, Salary $3150, Min $2865, Mid $3180, Max $3500 (Equal)

JG8, Exec Secretary, 1, Salary $2840, Min $2365, Mid $2630, Max $2890 (+20%)

JG8, Sales Staff, 4, Salary $2840, Min $2365, Mid $2630, Max $2890(+20%)

JG8, Training Staff, 2, Salary $2840, Min $2365, Mid $2630, Max $2890(+20%)

JG7, Secretary, 3, Salary $2045, Min $1900, $2110, $2320(-10%)

JG6, Pack/Ship Asst, 20, Salary $1855, Min $1545, Mid $1720, Max $1890(+20%)

JG6, Accounts Staff, 4, Salary $1855, Min $1545, Mid $1720, Max $1890(+20%)

JG6, Services Staff, 3, Salary $1505, Min $1545, Mid $1720, Max $1890(+15/20%)

JG6, Receptionist/Oprt, 2, Salary $1855, Min $1545, Mid $1720, Max $1890(+20%)

JG5, Maint Mechanic, 6, Salary $1510, Min $1260, Mid $1400, Max $1540(+20%)

JG5, Electrician, 2, Salary $1510, Min $1260, Mid $1400, Max $1540(+20%)

JG5, Warehouse Asst, 2, Salary $1510, Min $1260, Mid $1400, Max $1540(+20%)

JG4, Forklift Oprt, 2, Salary $1230, Min $1020, Mid $1135, Max $1245(+20%)

JG4, Quality Cont F/man, 16, Salary $1230, Min $1020, Mid $1135, Max $1245(+20%)

JG4, Nurse/Driver, 3, Salary $1230, Min $1020, Mid $1135, Max $1245 (+20%)

JG 3, Security Guard, 7, Salary $925, Min $830,Mid $920, Max $1015(Equal)

JG 2, Cook, 2, Salary $750, Min $675, Mid $750, Max $825(Equal)

JG 1, Shift Worker, 72, Salary $545, Min $545, Mid $605, Max $665

JG 1, Cleaner, 6, Salary $545, Min $545, Mid $605, Max $665

Total Employees 177

Since we now know exactly how difficult (or easier) our own jobs are compared to those of the market, we can pay the right salary for the right job.

The SOFI Corporation is now ready to start its most critical phase the setting up the company; that of recruiting the family made up of its people. This is the most important step for any company because it virtually means that you have to live with your decisions and the people you choose for as long as the company is in existence.

Without perhaps realizing it at this stage, you and your team are now primarily and directly responsible for creating the culture of the company itself. People really do make all the difference.

The next chapter focuses on the critical task of locating, identifying, interviewing and hiring the right people for your company.

CHAPTER 7
Recruitment, Interview and Employment

There are benefits in using recruitment agencies because they can sometimes save time by doing the initial screening of candidates on your behalf.

You have decided to use a reputable recruitment agency for your initial requirement for the start-up staffing of SOFI Corporation in Turkey. Several advertisements were placed in prominent journals and newspapers informing the public about the general activities of the SOFI group.

As a result, there has been some favorable publicity in the press announcing the proposed establishment of your plant.

You have arranged for translations of the promotional SOFI Group booklet describing the activities of the company, its operations, the advantages that it offers to its employees and the opportunities for employment with the SOFI group, emphasizing a lifetime career for the right people.

You are convinced of the value of praising your company. Some of the information, for all applicants in the booklet will contain such items as:

- What do we manufacture? **Top quality appliances that are already very popular in Europe and US**
- What will be your job? **You will contribute to our work in assembling the top quality modern electronic household appliances in a pleasant and safe workplace**

- Do you need to have previous experience? **No. SOFI Corporation has an excellent orientation and training program that is geared to help you to meet our company objective by enhancing your capabilities in all areas.**

- What do we offer? **Basically, we offer you enjoyable work in a clean and comfortable workplace with congenial fellow employees. Coupled with your keenness in promoting our mutual goals, we assure you an enjoyable lifetime career with good pay and excellent benefits.**

Recruitment startup

Our immediate priority is to arrange that the following interim key positions are taken on board as soon as possible. The 27 jobs for immediate hire are marked in parentheses in the total company-manning table given hereunder:

***

Factory production (2x8 hour shifts)	Shift Worker 72	Shift Foreman 16 (6)	Shift Eng 8	Packing/Shipping Assistants 20	Safety Eng 4	Prod Manager 2	Total 122
Factory Support (3x8 hour shifts)	Maintenance Mechanic 6 (2)	Electrician 2 (1)	Warehouse Asst 2	Forklift Operator 2	Security 7 (4)	Cleaners 6 (2)	Total 25
Normal Operations- (9 hours x5day week)	Receptionist/ Operator 2 (1)	Cooks 2	Secretaries 3 (3)	Accts Staff 4 (2)	Sales Staff 4 Training Staff 2	Services Staff (2) 3	Total 18
Normal Operations-Management (9 hours x5day week)	Marketing Manager 1	Finance Manager (1)	Personnel Management Director (1)	Legal/PR Manager (1)	Plant Manager (1)	General Manager (1)	Total 6
Medical Support Training	Doctor 1 Trainer 2	Nurse & Ambulance Driver 3(1)					Total 4 2
TOTAL							177

A cardinal principle is that it is easier to hire additional employees later than it is to let go employees who were taken on board in too much haste and later found to be above the actual requirement.

The advantage of using the services of a good recruitment agency is that they will make all the needed arrangements for pre-screening and reference checks of the suitable candidates. In all probability, you may need to only interview one or two of the most suitable short-listed candidates. Furthermore, the interview would be conducted in suitable premises arranged by the recruitment agency.

Once the start up team has joined the company, there is then ample time to recalculate projections, design relevant tests if needed in recruitment and to prepare the proper advertisements. In general, the start up phase is that of readying the operational facilities for full-time plant activity.

The Sofi Corporation policy will conclude **fixed-term annual contracts** with its employees for the first year of service with confirmation after one year of service.

The recruitment process

Local hiring of the 72 shift workers will be left until the last phase and when all of the company staff has been taken on board.

The recruitment team should preferably include the Personnel Management Director, the Plant Manager or his delegate and one of the Services Assistants. Advertisements for the jobs need to appear in at least two major daily newspapers in each of the major industrial cities for a period of 2 days and should give some basic information about the Company and location of its factory. Arrangements will need to be made with a suitable and major 5-star hotel to host these interviews.

Details of each job should be outlined in the advertisement requesting interested candidates to pickup a copy of the SOFI Corporation information booklet together with the application form from the hotel. A telephone contact number must appear in the advertisement needed to call for an appointment after filling in the application form.

The application form

Almost all companies use application forms and which are usually taken from those used by other companies.

A recent study made of the various types of employment application forms has shown that the most of them have been drawn up spontaneously without much thought into the values of its use. Here are some items that may need to be included in the form, which should have a recent photograph:

- Full name (maiden name in case of married ladies)
- Full present address and period (Also previous address if less than 2 years)
- Age and date of birth (Place of birth is not needed)
- Military service (If male and if in a country with conscription)
- Marital status (If married is spouse employed, where and number of children)
- Education (Name and place of schools, graduations dates)
- Language skills (Which languages, level of reading, writing, speaking)
- Foreign residence (List countries if more than 6 months in duration)
- Work experience (Title of job, name of employer, location and duration)

- Other skills (Such as ability and level of computer usage, driving licenses, other)
- Name and address of two references

The form may also ask the following questions:

- Do you have any close relatives working for the company?
- Do you have any restrictions to traveling (air, sea, land)
- Will you be able to undergo training courses if needed in other cities or other countries?

Statement: I certify that the above is true to the best of my knowledge and that in the event of my employment, that I will fully abide with conflict of interest policies of the company. (Applicant should sign the form.)

The job interview

This is the most critical part of the employment process. Before the interview, a pre-assessment of objectives is essential and this session needs to be chaired by the CEO or the General Manager.

Recent research overwhelmingly indicates that many good and well-suited candidates are "lost" in a novice interview.

Here are a few tips that can help:

- Make sure you are familiar with the job. Study the 1-page job description.
- Read the candidate's application form before the meeting.
- Privacy is important; in fact it is a must. The

room must be comfortable, quiet, well lighted and spacious so that it can have a good impression on the candidate.

- It is difficult to plan an interview from the beginning. Take control of the interview from the beginning and use a checklist to briefly note down the answers.

- Try to keep your interview time to a standard; not too short and not too long.

- If you decide to hire him or her, he or she has ample time to listen to you most of the time in future and probably won't be able to talk to you at all; this is their only chance to talk to you, so put the applicant at ease and listen.

- I surprise myself every single day when I learn something new about the oddness of my personality and wonder whether I really do know myself all that well. The hardest thing on earth is to get to know someone else well. My advice is to focus solely on the job requirements and not to go beyond judging whether or not you'd really enjoy being in the company of that person almost every day in the future.

- End the interview by inviting potential candidates to the company plant for final employment decisions.

The employment process

- Reference checks
- Medical exams
- Legally binding employment contracts
- Probationary trial periods
- Orientation programs for all newcomers

CHAPTER 8
Manpower costs

The SOFI Corporation is now ready to go on stream and all needed manpower has been taken on board. But what has this all going to cost? Here is the answer:

<u>Sofi Corporation Total Payroll ($per month)</u>

JG 13, Gen Mgr, ($6550-$7300-$6040) 1 x $12,445=$12455

JG 12, Plant Mgr, ($5330- $5935-$6535) 1 x $8530=$8530

JG 11, Marketing Mgr, ($4330-$4825-$5320) 1 x $5630=$5630

JG 11, Prod Mgr, ($4330-$4825-$5320) 2 x $5630=$11260

JG 10, Personnel Director, ($3580-$4000- $4370) 1 x $3560=$3560

JG 10, Legal/PR Mgr, ($3580-$4000- $4370) 1 x $3560=$3560

JG 10, Finance Mgr, ($3580-$4000- $4370) 1 x $3560=$3560

JG9, Safety Engineer, ($2865-$3180-$3500) 4x $3150=$12600

JG9, Quality Cont Eng, ($2865-$3180-$3500) 8x $3150=$25200

JG9, Doctor, ($2865-$3180-$3500) 1x $3150=$3150

JG8, Exec Secretary, ($2365- $2630- $2890) 1 x $2840=$2840

JG8, Sales Staff, ($2365- $2630- $2890) 4 x $2840=$11360

JG8, Training Staff, ($2365- $2630- $2890) 2 x $2840=$5680

JG7, Secretary, ($1900- $2110- $2320) 3x $2045=$6135

JG6, Pack/Ship Asst, ($1545-$1720-$1890) 20x $1855=$37100

JG6, Accounts Staff, ($1545-$1720-$1890) 4x $1855=$7420

JG6, Services Staff, ($1545-$1720-$1890) 3x $1505=$4515

JG6, Receptionist/Oprt, ($1545-$1720-$1890) 2x $1855=$3710

JG5, Maint Mechanic, ($1260- $1400-$1540) 6 x $1510=$9060

JG5, Electrician, ($1260- $1400-$1540) 2 x $1510=$3020

JG5, Warehouse Asst, ($1260- $1400-$1540) 2 x $1510=$3020

JG4, Forklift Oprt, ($1020- $1135- $1245) 2x $1230=$2460

JG4, Quality Cont F/man, ($1020- $1135- $1245) 16x $1230=$19680

JG4, Nurse/Driver, ($1020- $1135- $1245) 3x $1230=$3690

JG 3, Security Guard, ($925- $830- $920) 7x$760=$5320

JG 2, Cook, ($675-$750-$825) 2 x $750=$1500

JG 1, Shift Worker, ($545-$605-$665) 72x $545=$39240

JG 1, Cleaner, ($545-$605-$665) 6x $545=$3270

Total Employees 177   Total Payroll $258525

In addition to salaries that are paid directly to employees, companies also need to pay out fairly high overheads as well. Unless these costs are carefully tracked, they can easily evade even the closest scrutiny and it is possible to lose control of what the exact manpower cost has come to. Unfortunately, despite the fact that most companies have good financial control techniques, the fact is that most of them experience difficulties in this area.

Here is what the total manpower costs of the SOFI Corporation actually add up to:

The basic monthly average salary is $1461 (Company total monthly payroll, $258525, divided by 177 employees).

SOFI Corporation provides

- $208 per month cost of free meals per employee
- $200 free transport per month per employee
- Protective/uniform clothing issued once every 6 months at cost of $ 2000 per year
- Employer share of social insurance premiums (medical, retirement and accident)

Basic Average Salary per Month	Bonuses	Free Meals per Person	Free Transport Per Person	Clothing per Person	Social Insurance Employer Share per Person	Total Manpower Cost per Person	Total Company Manpower Cost per Month	Total Company Manpower Cost per Year
$1461	0	$208	$200	$167	$212	$2248	$397,896	$4,774,752 -$ 72,216* $4,702,536
*Less Meals and Transport during July								

The SOFI Corporation has not provided any excessive perks and no bonuses have been paid. Yet its overheads have come to over 54% of the basic payroll.

So that the importance of the manpower costs can be seen

in this context, it needs to be looked at as a component of total production costs.

The SOFI Corporation had been basically set up as an "outsourcing" operation to supply the following annual products required for the company's emerging markets in the Black Sea and Caspian region.

The sales revenues have therefore been predetermined:

***

ANNUAL REVENUE

	DAILY	MONTHLY	YEARLY		SALES
HOUSEHOLD IRONS	2000	60000		660,000	$11,880,000
COOLER-HEATER WATER FOUNTAIN	1000	30000		330,000	$29,040,000
HAIR CONDITIONER	2000	60000		660,000	$5,280,000
				TOTAL	$46,200,000

ANNUAL COSTS

10-year loan repayment	Annual premise lease fees	Total Fixed and Variable production costs (Non manpower)	Total payroll and overheads	Total costs per year
$8,800,000	$850,000	$13,900,000	$4,702,536	$28,252,536

The SOFI Corporation investment would yield:

Total Sales	$ 46,200,000
Less Total Costs	$ 28,252,536
Pre-tax profit	$17,946,464
Less 20% Corporate tax	$-3,589,293
Net Return on Investment	$14,357,717 (17.95%)

The SOFI Corporation total payroll at startup was <u>16.66%</u> of total annual cost .

PART III
GOOD EMPLOYEE MANAGEMENT

CHAPTER 9
Manpower cost controls

As outlined in the previous chapter, one particular area that definitely requires careful monitoring is that of manpower cost controls.

Every now and then we read of massive layoffs by the giant corporations.

The Economist recently reviewed a new book titled DRIVING DOWN COSTS- How to manage and cut costs Intelligently by Andrew Wileman. As it is certainly relevant to this subject, the ECONOMIST excerpt is quoted hereunder:

"Mr Wileman begins flatteringly enough: "**The Economist** had it right the first time: Cost management is not just for downturns but for always.

" Downturns certainly help focus managers' minds, especially when the spectre of redundancy haunts the office corridors. Being one of the hardest costs to keep down, headcount should be assessed as a capital expense, he says, with salaries and associated costs discounted several years down the line, not least because it can be hellishly difficult to shift underperformers."

There are several payroll expense control techniques now available but in my opinion, a relatively user-friendly and short-cut formula called COMPA-RATIO devised by Edward N. Hay is still one of the easiest and most popular systems in use today.

The Compa-ratio tool can be used not only to monitor where each employee is within his/her salary range but also as an expense control tool.

Assume you would like to look at salary grade 2, with a total of 5 employees.

The range for salary grade 2 is $1000-$1500-$2000. ($1000 is minimum paid on the market, $1500 is the market average and the top salary of $2000 is the maximum paid for that job in the market). There is a difference of $1000 between the lowest and the highest salary.

The 5 employees in grade 2 are paid monthly salaries as shown hereunder:

$1400
$1800
$1950
$2200
$2250

To calculate a compa-ratio for salary grade 2, please do the following:

Add salaries of all 5 employees in grade: (1400+1800+1950+2200+2250)$9600

Divide by the medium of range: 1500   = 6.4

A compa-ratio of 6.4 tells us that the company pays just 5 of its employees the salary equivalent of 6.4 people earning the market average. In other words the company has grossly overpaid some of its staff.

It is also a good idea to constantly check the total Compa-ratio for the whole company on a regular basis and "keep a finger on the pulse".

The following example is for a company-wide Compa-ratio calculation:

Assume there are only 4 grades in the company:

		Salary Range	
	Min	Mid	Max
Grade 1	$940	$1045	$1150
Grade 2	$1160	$1290	$1420
Grade 3	$1430	$1590	$1750
Grade4	$1760	$1955	$2150

Here are the total salaries for each of the grades divided by the grade midpoint:

Gr1: $\frac{(800+ 900 +12800)\ 14500}{1045} = 13.88$ (16 employees)

Gr2: $\frac{(1400+1250+1700)4350}{1290} = 3.37$ (3 employees)

Gr3: $\frac{(2000+2250+2300)6550}{1590} = 4.12$ (3 employees)

Gr4: $\frac{(2200+4800+2700)9700}{1955} = 4.96$ (4 employees)

Next add the compa-ratios found for all the grades:

$13.88 + 3.37 + 4.12 + 4.96 = \underline{26.33.}$

Dividing 26.33 by the number of employees (16+3+3+4) 26 = 1.013 x 100= 101. This is the compa-ratio for the whole organization. A 100 rating would have meant that all the employees were being paid the market average.

This seems to good news from the point of payroll expense controls as it means that all of your employees are paid almost exactly the market average pay.

However, when the individual compa-ratios for job grades are looked at:

• There are 16 employees in grade 1 but they are all

underpaid- their total wages less than that paid in the market for only 14 employees.

- There is no problem in grade 2.
- There are only 3 people in grade 3 but they are overpaid; they earn the pay of 4 employees.
- There is over payment in grade 4 as well; only 4 people here but paid the salaries of 5 employees.

The Compa-ratio tool alerts you to potential wage inequality problems that could later fester into unrest and problems for you if they not addressed.

CHAPTER 10
The Hygiene Factors

The good company needs to critically look at what has become known as 'hygiene' factors. What exactly are they?

The Wikipedia Encyclopedia quotes the Hygiene factors, developed by Frederick Herzberg in his work related to motivation, as being job factors that can cause dissatisfaction if missing, but do not necessarily motivate employees if increased.

The company needs to look at its own organization in this light and learn about:

- How the business is organized - is it hierarchical, formal, informal, relaxed, a fearsome intimidating place to work etc?

- Pay - is pay appropriate to the job of work being carried out?

- Do workers see their pay as being fair?

- Status - how do people see themselves in the organization? Do they feel they have some respect - whatever job it is they do?
- Job security - do people feel secure as far as their job is concerned or are they constantly worried about losing their job or being made redundant?

- The way leaders and managers treat the workforce and react with them

- Working conditions - is the working environment too hot, too cold, too noisy, are the chairs uncomfortable, is it cramped, too dark, too light, etc.

- Work relationships - how do people get on with each other?

CHAPTER 11
Policies, cost controls and delegations of financial authority

The SOFI Corporation is fortunate that the new company is able to readily adapt parent company policies and procedures to a local context.

All employees, regardless of level should be made aware of the company vision and its ground rules and matters related to conflict of interest spelt out. As a rule, companies issue manuals for this purpose, outlining company policy in simple terms for the information and the guidance of its employees.

Budgetary cost control is a vital part of all company operations. Actual expenditures must be compared against budgets and needs to be closely monitored on a monthly basis by a management accounts unit. Although budget cost controls statements are usually in arrears, it is the most effective cost control tool available.

Financial authority delegation must be made for effective control of disbursements and payments.

Internal audits will need to be conducted at regular intervals. The SOFI Corporation had arranged for the parent company auditors to conduct needed assessments.

CHAPTER 12
Employee Performance Appraisal

Pros and cons

So much is being said for or against employee performance ratings that it makes any reasonable statement on this subject highly difficult.

I expect that in the final analysis, an acid test would turn out to be in favor of doing employee ratings as opposed to not doing any at all.

On the pro side, ratings appear to be the only tool for managers and supervisors to:

- Allow them to see the real differences between all their staff.
- Understand employee aspirations and to discuss their strong and weak points.
- Serve as a record of accomplishment, merit increases and basis for promotions.
- Serve as a basis for training and development on the job.
- To uncover exceptional talents and to identify potential managers.
- Ratings also shed light on each of the rating supervisor's style of management
- Finally and most importantly, it can improve

employee morale by stimulating confidence in the fairness of Management

On the negative side though:

- Managers and supervisors really look at staff appraisals as a necessary evil that must be done at a sacrifice of valuable time needed for their more important work
- The overwhelming tendency is to find a way to rate nearly 90% of staff as "average"
- All ratings are clearly subjective with a lot of emotion involved and not systematic
- Despite their best efforts at trying to be fair, almost all managers and supervisors only have a very rough estimate of the capabilities and potential of their staff.
- The American writer Thomas Arthur Ryan said, rightly so, that rating must be taken on faith as there is really no way of testing their validity.
- Many writers sharply criticize the use of performance rating as a basis for merit increases. Some have pointed out that the raters even had the overall production records available and actually used them to correlate to the ratings.
- In employee opinion surveys

    - 75% said rating is of little or no use
    - 52% say they shouldn't be used in promotions
    - 70% said ratings help the company and only 10% said it helps employees
    - Overwhelmingly, the opinion was that raters do not know the employee sufficiently well.

The need for employee appraisal

However, although there are weaknesses and limitations, highly improved rating methods are now universally used in industry as the genuine and overwhelming need for objective measures in assessing employee performance has pushed the development of new techniques in appraisal.

In this relation, the Shell Group many years ago introduced the use of a novel concept, that of "balancing extremes" in performance rating. This was proven to be highly successful in achieving reasonable staff ratings. This concept is now also used by Motorola and several other large corporations

The system essentially assesses how successful the employee was in the exercise of certain qualities while maintaining a desired state of balance in achieving objectives.

For example, balance in assessing knowledge is that

- If the knowledge has too much depth, balance can deteriorate into the knowledge becoming too detailed and specific in that the employee is not too knowledgeable in other subjects
- If on the other hand, the knowledge has too much spread, then balance can deteriorate into the knowledge becoming too limited or too shallow, such as "jack of all trades and master of none".

If balance is being assessed in decision-making, then

- If decision-making is too decisive, then balance can deteriorate into stubbornness
- If decision-making becomes too flexible, then balance can deteriorate into capriciousness

Another quality for balance is

- If employee is too much of an individualist, balance can deteriorate into egotism
- If employee is too cooperative then the balance could deteriorate into dependence

The Shell appraisal system actually then also appraises the rater as well.

There are a great variety of ratings systems being used. Some of the larger corporations use systems they have themselves devised and judge them to be the best for use in the context of their own company culture. Some rating systems that are known to be used:

- Horizontal ratings by fellow-employees
- Joint management and labor union rating of employees
- Ranking of individual employees known to the rater from highest to lowest
- Paired comparison ratings by a group, who each separately rate sets of 2 names each answering "who is better" and compare the findings to reach a standard score
- Forced Distribution System, devised by Joseph Tiffin to assess only two factors, that of performance and of promotability. The Tiffin system used a five-step scale for performance and asked raters to place the employee into 1) Lowest 10%, 2) Next 20%, Mid 40%, Next 20% and Highest 10%. For promotability Tiffin uses only three scales: 1) Most likely to be promoted 2) May or may not be promoted and 3) Not likely to be promoted.
- An American writer, Reign H. Bittner, describes a technique called "Forced-choice". This essentially uses several sets of four statements, each taken from the employee's job description.

Two of these statements are favorable and the other two unfavorable. Let us assume this trait is that of productivity:

1.   Does more than his share of the work
2.   Turns our inferior work
3.   Exceeds his work quote
4.   Is late in turning out the work

The rater must chose 2 statements of each set. One statement must MOST describe the employee's productivity and the other statement must be LEAST descriptive of the employee's work.

The problem is that both of the favorable statements appear to be the same. Similarly the unfavorable statements too appear to be similar. The difficulty by the rater is the force choice of only one. According to Bittner, the system allows for cross validation of the rating.

Performance rating as a means of identifying deadwood?

Yes, indeed. Research into new performance appraisal systems can accommodate the sad eventuality of redundancies in future.

Massive layoffs are regularly happening in downsizing or for other reasons. The tragic part of layoffs is that top potential people get on the same chopping block as the deadwood.

Thinking out loud: it could make sense to carry a system allowing for a set degree of marginal under-performers to continue for periods of say, 3-4 years in a row so that a "bank" of potential under-performers can be built and identified.

All companies have their own deadwood problems. Keeping this to a maximum of 10% may be livable limit for most companies. It's always good to have a little "fat" to spare.

CHAPTER 13
Job promotions and job transfers

Promotion from within is preferable to the option of bringing new people into the organization, unless there are exceptional and overriding reasons such as setting up new functions within the company.

This option however is really the difficult one, because an obvious easy choice for any manager is to be able to fill any vacancy by advertising for the job.

Promotion essentially means increased responsibility and a higher status with better pay. Therefore, competition for the higher-ranking job is almost certain and it can become fierce unless there is a clear policy outlining the steps in a fair and objective system based on merit or on seniority within the organization. Clearly, periodic performance appraisal rating is one of the tools for such a system.

Company policy should clearly spell out the management prerogative to make a final decision as to whether or not new people will be recruited to fill vacancies.

Transfers within the organization also need to be spelt out in the scope of the company policy. Although internal transfers are not really higher-ranking jobs, the competition for perceived desirable jobs can occur.

Internal transfers in all organizations are necessary. Some reasons for this are:

- Training employees for exposure to different jobs.
- Relieving monotony, providing creativity and motivation
- To correct erroneous placement (wrong people in job)
  - Temporary "fill-in" of jobs for holiday replacement, production changes, etc

Company policy regarding internal transfers should also spell out the management prerogatives.

CHAPTER 14
Training

In the SOFI Corporation example, the main responsibility of the local training support unit is to provide basic orientation activities for all new staff and to coordinate arrangements for bookings to training seminars and courses for selected staff at the parent company training center in Geneva.

Training is necessary if you have a need to upgrade the skill level of your employees or in the event that it is necessary for your business to be on par with the latest technology.

On the other hand, should it be that your company plans to set up a totally new operation, then it is very likely that simply training your present employees to perform new jobs could be a waste of time.

In general, any form of job training simply cannot upgrade the skill and educational level of most of your present employees. The answer, in this case would be to hire new people who do have the needed skills, despite the higher cost and effort involved in a recruitment campaign.

Clearly, an accurate assessment of employee skill levels in your own company is essential. But then this does depend on your managers actually knowing the skill levels of their own staff.

Many of the top companies say that because they have frequent performance ratings, they do know the skill levels of their employees. The problem here is that as performance can never be an objective assessment, the skill levels could tend to be inflated, or conversely severely downgraded.

My experience is that many companies, even those who do frequent performance ratings, <u>DO NOT KNOW</u> their employees, or their individual skill levels well enough.

All companies need annual training plans to tie in with the timing of performance ratings. The first step in finding out accurate employee skill levels can however only is made through a direct survey of employees.

The finding of this initial survey will most likely highlight future training needs for the whole organization and allow the development of annual training plans.

As a prime authority has said, "Training is more than a putting-out-the-fire approach". The classic and accepted formula for determining training is

Job Requirements - employee's present skills = TRAINING NEEDS

CHAPTER 15
Succession Planning and Management Development

Although all the large corporations have some form of succession planning programs, not even two of them use the same methods.

Many CEO's believe that the only viable tool to identify management talent is through well-balanced employee performance ratings and the interviews that go along with the rating exercise.

The likelihood that any untested potential candidate can bypass the critical point of identification as "executive material" at these joint discussions can be very high.

High subjectivity is at work here simply because the manager is keen to "discover" potential and equally, the candidate is keen that this does happen.

A time-honored system that has worked for hundreds of years in many reputable companies is the practice of temporary appointment of different candidates to similar higher positions to observe their performance.

An acid test comparison between potential executive candidates clearly reveals that there is no discernible difference between any of the best performers who fall in the top 20%.

My personal experience of some 30 years of work in three world-class international corporations corroborates these findings.

Most international corporations carefully plot and plan career programs for identified future executives and arrange expensive training seminars and international rotational job assignments in other countries.

More than frequently, there is then much anguish when carefully "groomed" potential managers suddenly leave the company for better-paying executive positions with competitor corporations.

This is the patch of the "head-hunters", who are paid huge sums for "arranging" these job transfers.

Small family-owned companies have traditionally "groomed" their own younger generation for the top jobs and they do generally succeed. Their clear advantage is that the younger generation usually continues with the family culture and traditions in the company. Company success has been closely related to employee content in these family-owned companies, who are all happy that they stand to gain with the younger management.

CHAPTER 16
The Wage market survey in the community

You may have started off with good salaries and wages compared to the market but it is possible that your pay could now be below that of the market. The best way of finding out is doing your own market salary survey every 2-3 years. You need to:

1. Identify your "benchmark" jobs. These are all the jobs in your company that are easily comparable with those in companies similar to yours. For example, drivers are about the same. Secretaries could however significantly differ; for other companies may call their receptionists "secretary".

2. Compare apples with apples and oranges with oranges. Make sure that you include all the fringes and bonus payments for your company and for that the other company. Watch out however for the odd participating company that will try to conceal their real wages or fringes.

- The mean average of the community becomes the midpoints of your new job grades.

- Make sure that confidentiality is maintained with the participating companies and that you only identify each other with coded references, not by actual company names. The participating companies will appreciate this gesture.

CHAPTER 17
Brave New World: the specter of employee unrest

E mployee unrest can start suddenly and usually takes management by surprise when it is too late to have taken simple action to prevent it.

Surprisingly, it mostly happens in corporations who have over-efficient managers who tend to "put out the minor fire" and manage it all on their own.

Unrest has an uncanny tendency to infect colleague employees to "group" behavior, which eventually can lead to uncontrollable "crowd" behavior.

Watch carefully for these signs:

- Job dissatisfaction and derogatory comments.
- Daydreaming.
- Frequent lateness.
- Too-frequent medical visits, absenteeism and other

Dealing with employee unrest is the forte of talented management. People want to be told the "ground rules" and just issuing a well-prepared policy manual is not going to do it. Company vision needs to be expressed verbally.

FACE-TO-FACE CONTACTS
Why is it that face-to-face communication <u>always</u> works

wonders and that almost always, impersonally written curt letters, emails or circulars containing important information turns people "off".

Categorically, employees only look positively at brief written messages to seek simple information, such as announcing dates of wage or other payments, or similar information. Anything that goes beyond these simple concepts should not be communicated in writing and needs the personal touch.

Not enough can be said for the magic and the value of a "personal touch".

THE PERSONAL TOUCH

There is simply no alternative to "making yourself visible". There has been much written about the need for top managers to simply "talk" to employees at all levels and I too, make a strong appeal to managers not too allow this opportunity to vanish.

The very nature of human beings is that everyone loves authority and will compete to be near to and to obey authority.

A clinical research in this regard was conducted by Professor Stanley Milligram at a US Mid Western university many years ago. He published as a book entitled **OBEDIENCE TO AUTHORITY** to outline the research.

While not overdoing it, an informal chat visit to the shop floors could work wonders for your company through positively enhanced employee moral.

Here are some pointers that could be useful:

- Try to get to know employees by their names.
- Ask about their private lives and let them talk. As they are a group, the talk will not be too lengthy

because their colleagues too, have things to say to you and would cut the "talker" short.

- Make a note of potential problem areas. This is not a promise of any action or a sign of concern. If it is significant enough, bring this to the attention of your managers or take action.
- Do not be put off by assuming that through talking to all level of company employees, you have made yourself accessible. Remember that it is not easy to penetrate the well protected privacy of your office and your secretary is not likely allow unscheduled visitors.
- Employees will highly respect you for showing them this basic courtesy.
- Last but certainly not least, **smile.**

President Dwight Eisenhower won two difficult US elections by landslides. According to a Time Magazine news account at the time, General Eisenhower's ex-aide from the European World War II arena, a Sergeant who had served with the General during the war helped him with his phenomenal memory for faces and names.

He accompanied Ike everywhere during the presidential campaigns. Even when Ike stopped over at out-of-the-mainstream different locations in the US, Ike would surprise people that he had met only once by addressing them by name and even asked about their families and children by name. Eisenhower's aide had whispered all their names to him just before meeting them.

DO PRACTICE:

- Coaching, periodic performance rating and exit interviews of staff leaving you.

- Publish professional and interesting company histories (in cartoon form)
- Start and encourage suggestion systems that give out high monetary rewards
- Arrange social events for employees and families (cocktails, picnics)
- Have a team organize "Fun" sports activities for employees and families

WHAT HAPPENS IF YOU ALLOW UNREST

- Work stoppages and "slow-downs", or even mass protests
- High rate of defective production
- Lapses in quality standards
- Total loss of motivation
- Possible loss in your balance sheet.

PART IV
BACK TO THE SOFI CORP SCENARIO

CHAPTER 18
November

It has now been almost three months since production started during the second week of August. I must admit that I am becoming quite fond of my home away from home and find myself reflecting on recent developments within the pastoral quiet of my tastefully furnished office. My second floor office window faces a pleasant line of trees.

These months have not been uneventful. A few changes had become necessary in the composition of our staff and 17 of our shift workers had either resigned or had been released for violation of safety rules or because they had not been able to adapt to rigorous production schedules.

One major change that was the most difficulty decision for me was in the need to replace the finance manager about a month ago. Although he had been just the right person for us and had set up a highly efficient well-functioning accounts department within a very short time, he had been offered a senior job with a major corporation and gave notice to leave the company.

Two internal candidates had applied for this job.

One candidate was the outgoing Finance Manager's senior assistant in the accounting department. He has had about 8 years' experience in the accounts of several major pharmaceutical companies. He spoke fairly good English and seemed to be well suited for the job. The only problem was that the outgoing manager had not recommended him for the job.

I thought that a possible reason for this was that they had only worked with each other for a fairly short time and that this had been a natural reaction.

The other candidate was one of the two training support staff, a talented young lady whose husband works as the local manager of the bank in the nearby town. She not only spoke excellent English but was also fluent in French, a definite asset in our communications with the Geneva head office.

The Personnel Director however had recommended that the company recruits an external candidate. His reasoning was that as we had not yet commissioned an overall performance appraisal system for the company, a promotion of this level could be premature and would not be based on real operational requirements.

I have agreed with this rationale and have advertised for this position. It has now been filled by a promising finance manager who not only speaks excellent English but is also a registered chartered accountant.

December

Two major items have taken up our agenda. One had been the need to urgently revise earlier cost estimates to reflect rises in operating and essential raw material prices, expected to increase by 7.3% as of the new year.

Total non-manpower costs will therefore increase from $13,900,000 to $14,910,00 as of the beginning of the next year and means that the overall cost will increase by 3.5% for the year. The board has approved this inevitable increase. The expected return on investment will now be about 16.94%.

There is no possibility for us or for the parent company

to reflect these increases on to the product because of the assurance extended to emerging markets that the SOFI parent Corporation would hold its prices firm until the beginning of the coming year.

The second major item is in a more pleasant vein. I just met with the company recreation committee and reviewed their plans for the first New Year's company party for all its employees and their families. I discovered that there are a total of 566 employees and family members.

I approved a total outlay of $18,000 for the New Year party, which will be held at the town's major hotel. This is quite suitable because the majority of our employees live in the town area.

I do have plans to eventually setup a recreation center within company premises for company employees and their families. Our head office however has deemed this to be premature and has not approved my initial proposal.

January

The company party on New Year's Eve was a huge success. All employees were given two days off to prepare for the New Year. The monthly salaries were paid early that month and the mood was radiant throughout.

The CEO of the group himself and two senior members of the board in Geneva attended the party. The CEO's brief speech, which was translated, was welcomed by the employees.

We were visited by the inspectors from the labor Ministry, mainly to ensure that legal safety requirements had been met. We were congratulated for the SOFI Corporation's traditional stance on safety and health issues and for implementing strict safety procedures.

One minor problem that we encountered was that we had apparently not abided by the legal requirement to hire our quota of disabled persons and ex-convicts. We were given a small fine for the violation and notified to deal with this matter as early as possible.

February

One of our cleaners and a cook's helper suddenly resigned. At this early stage, I am particularly interested in all details, no matter how minor or insignificant. My previous experience has proven that totally effective management control can only be achieved by meticulous attention to all details at the very start of operations; nothing is too unimportant and I admit that I am still at a learning stage here.

The labor ministry directorate provided us with listings of ex-convict and disabled applicants and we have now hired two ex-convicts to fill both of the jobs.

Frankly, I am pleasantly surprised to observed how grateful both our new employees are in their new jobs; precisely the kind of motivation I am keen for!

March

March turned out to be a month of surprises for all of us.

First of all, our shipments were rather sharply disrupted because of the sudden closure of the main railway line due to preliminary work related to Turkey's new fast-train railway project.

This 2-week railway closure affected our shipping logistics to the extent of heavy build-up of product at the warehouses and at the end of the first week, crates had needed to be stored outdoors with makeshift plastic covering in the likelihood of rain.

At one stage, it began to look like we would run out of outdoor space as well. Fortunately however, we were able to reach a deal with a large international shipping company who immediately arranged interim trucking for most of the product stored outdoors.

The second surprise turned out to be a visit by a national Turkish trade union who told us that their union now represented the majority of our employees.

The union will now need to confirm this claim with an official notification from the government labor directorate. In the meantime, we also need to ascertain this claim ourselves. Candidly, I was personally taken aback by such early union activity in our company, coming at a time that I thought was quite immature.

We discovered that 91 of our company employees had joined this union, which if officially confirmed by the labor authority, would allow the Union to start collective bargaining sessions.

Fortunately, none of our staff level employees had joined the union. According to the company figures, the following were now union members:

Shift workers	72
Main. Mechanic	6
Electrician	2
Forklift Operator	2
Cleaners	6
Nurse/Amb.Drv.	3
Total	91

I made arrangements for a staff cocktail party that weekend, to which all the factory production shift engineers, supervisors, safety officers and shift managers were also invited. This cocktail party proved to be quite productive and enlightening.

I had an excellent opportunity that evening to bring home to our employees the concept of out of scope staff policy and explained to them that any additional benefits granted to union members would be also be extended to them.

This of course created much excitement among our staff.

I then shared with them the need for the company to stay profitable. If this were not the case, then the only alternative would be to close shop, in which event everyone would suffer.

April

During the third part of the month, the Union visited us together with the government Labor Directorate, who submitted the official confirmation that this union was now authorized to negotiate a collective labor agreement.

The union requested to meet at the earliest opportunity and arrangements were made to meet with them on 8 May at the company premise.

The union stated that they would submit their demands to us during that meeting. We pointed out, in the presence of the labor director, that our company was a reputable international corporation with subsidies all over the world. We pointed out that our company was already paying highly competitive wages.

May

The union presented their demands to us during our first meeting. As I had expected, the demands were exorbitant.

We thanked the union and stated that at first sight, their demands appeared totally irresponsible and that this could only aim at stopping our industrial operation, which had just started up.

We arranged to meet again in ten days time, despite the union insistence to meet at an earlier date.

Our management team met that afternoon to review our present manpower costs.

Assuming that we had accepted all of the union demands, the overall manpower cost increase in percentage terms would have added 51.6% to the present payroll. Reflected in terms of overall return of investment, a manpower cost of $7,128,144 meant that the after-tax ROI would be $11,609,485 or a return of 14.51%.

When we met for the second time, we submitted the company proposal of a 10% wage increase and 15-day bonus as the absolute maximum that our management was prepared to allocate for manpower related costs. As expected, the union rejected our offer.

An unreal atmosphere had somehow started to envelope the previously friendly and positive relations with our employees in general. Frankly I am not too sure what had brought this about. I felt strained and slightly distrusting even to my closest colleagues.

The union has now also asked for severance indemnity to be paid to employees being terminated for reasons other than for cause, even though we had fixed-term work contracts with our employees.

The union rejected our counter proposal and asked that by the new week, the company table a better proposal. In return, we refused this request and asked them to let us have a more rational proposal, if that is, they were serious in continuing the negotiation.

We have now agreed to meet on the 28th of May for a final reckoning of our positions.

I and my wife departed to take a much-need vacation and to visit our children at boarding school. I will be meeting with the board in Geneva on 25th May.

GENEVA

The meeting of the board was most interesting, to say the least. In addition to myself, the meeting was attended by two members of the Asian equity finance group; literarily the owners of the company as such.

After much bantering during the session, which had become quite heated from time to time, the meeting was skillful handled by our CEO Francois Meyer and three options, two of which were quite viable, came out of the meeting.

Fortunately, I now have a bottom-line brief for a minimum return-of-investment of 14%. My brief now appears to be slightly easier to manage. Any agreement with the union must become effective for a period of 3 years as of the new-year, by which time the company will have posted a 12% product price increase. This also means that it will become easier to start implementing our group policy of good employee relations throughout the company.

***

THE MATCHBOOK ADVERTISING COMPANY

<u>ALTERNATIVE 1</u>

Basic Salary per month. (15% Increase)	No Bonus	Free Meals	Free Trans port	Clothing	15-day alloca-tion for possible sever-ance pay.	Social Insurance Employer Share. (14.5%)	Total Labor cost Per person per Month	Total Company Labor cost Per month	Total Company Manpower Cost per Year
1680	0	$208	$200	$250	$70	$243	$2651	$469,227	$5,630,724 -$72,216* $5,558,508

*Less cost of meals and transport during holiday month of July.

10-year loan repayment	Annual premise lease fees	Total Fixed and Variable production costs (Non manpower)	Total payroll and overheads	Total costs per year
$8,800,000	$850,000	$14,910,000	$5,558,508	$30,118,508

Total Sales	$ 46,200,000
Less Total Costs	$-30,118,508
Pre-tax profit	$16,081,492
Less 20% Corporate tax	$-3,216,298
Net Return on Investment	$12,865,194 (16.08%)

In the event that we are unable to reach an accord with the union, then our final resort would be the second option below.

***

ALTERNATIVE 2 (FINAL POSITION)

Basic Salary per month. (15% Increase)	15-day Bonus	Free Meals	Free Trans port	Clothing	15-day alloca-tion for possible sever-ance pay.	Social Insurance Employer Share. (14.5%)	Total Labor cost Per person per Month	Total Company Labor cost Per month	Total Company Manpower Cost per Year
$1680	$70	$208	$200	$250	$70	$254	$2732	$483,564	$5,802,768 -$72,216* $5,730,552

*Less cost of meals and transport during holiday month of July.

COSTS

10-year loan repayment	Annual premise lease fees	Total Fixed and Variable production costs (Non manpower)	Total payroll and overheads	Total costs per year
$8,800,000	$850,000	$14,910,000	$5,730,552	$30,290,552

RETURN ON INVESTMENT

Total Sales	$ 46,200,000
Less Total Costs	$-30,290,552
Pre-tax profit	$15,909,448
Less 20% Corporate tax	$-3,181,890
Net Return on Investment	$12,727,558 (15.91%)

ALTERNATIVE 3

The third alternative is much less attractive and not pleasant when looked at from the point of employment opportunity. I have been instructed to implement this option as the last resort and only in the event of an un-reconcilable deadlock with the union.

1. The company will scale down its production to working one shift 6 days per week.

2. A two-shift operation had required 56 people plus a relief backup of 16 employees to a total of 72 shift workers.

3. Recalculating the actual manpower needs for one 8-hour operation will now require 26 plus 6 backup relief employees, a total of 32 production workers.

4. As advised by the group legal unit, the work contracts

for all company employees will be amended to reflect indefinite period contracts, as defined in the labor law. This brings about the need to set aside an indemnity fund in the event it becomes necessary to pay termination benefits to any employee for severances other than for cause. Under the law, indemnity is not payable in the event of resignation. The board approved setting aside an allocation of 15 days pay per employee for this eventuality.

5.   This option will make 68 employees redundant (over 38% of the workforce). No separation indemnity is payable because of the fixed term 1-year contracts.

The product mix in our production will focus on more high-value items such as the popular heater-cooler water fountain towers, which are in high demand. We will be ready to conclude an agreement with the union for 3-years and may accept to a start date of 1 August.

	DAILY	MONTHLY	YEARLY	SALES
HOUSEHOLD IRONS	770	20000	220,000	$5,940,000
COOLER-HEATER WATER FOUNTAIN	1050	27,270	300,000	$26,400,000
HAIR CONDITIONER	1155	30000	330,000	$2,640,000
			TOTAL	$33,000,000

TOTAL MANPOWER COST (109 employees)

Basic Salary per month (15% increase)	15-day Bonus	Free Meals	Free Transport	Clothing	15-day allocation for possible severance pay.	Social Insurance Employer Share. (14.5%)	Total Labor cost Per person per Month	Total Company Labor cost Per month	Total Company Manpower Cost per Year
$1680	$70	$208	$200	$250	$70	$243	$2721	$296,589	$3,559,086 -$72,216* $3,486,852

*Less cost of meals and transport during holiday month of July.

TOTAL COSTS

10-year loan repayment	Annual premise lease fees	Total Fixed and Variable production costs (Non manpower)	Total payroll and overheads	Total costs per year
$8,800,000	$850,000	$7,455,000	$3,486,852	$20,591,852

RETURN ON INVESTMENT (Current year 1 August-31 December)

Total Sales	$ 33,000,000
Less Total Costs	$-20,591,852
Pre-tax profit	$12,408,148
Less 20% Corporate tax	$-2,481,630
Net Return on Investment	$9,926,518(12.41%)

RETURN ON INVESTMENT (1 January-31 December)

Total Sales	$ 36,960,000
Less Total Costs	$-20,591,852
Pre-tax profit	$16,368,148
Less 20% Corporate tax	$-3,273,630
Net Return on Investment	$13,094,518 (16.37%)

June

Our meeting with the union on 28 May was tumultuous, to say the least. A series of meetings continued throughout the month of June, with little progress on both sides.

The meeting on 16 June was subdued and was attended by several senior officials from the federation to which the union is affiliated.

At this meeting, we formally declared our intention of

releasing 68 of our employees by the end of the vacation month of July and to continue our operations as outlined in alternative 3.

The union officials had ample time to realize that our return of investment would actually be higher under the third alternative.

The president of the federation was a very experienced individual. He had a degree from a highly reputable French university and spoke excellent French and good English.

He invited my wife and me to his home in Ankara for dinner that weekend. We accepted this kind invitation and enjoyed a most cordial evening, our first in a Turkish home.

I could tell that a meeting of the minds was imminent. The president had already studied the history of our 53-year old group of companies and told me that it was a pleasure to deal with a company such as ours. I thanked him for his support.

The SOFI Corporation and the union signed a protocol on 28 June, with the president acting as a mediator between the parties. The collective agreement would become effective exactly as outlined in our alternative proposal 2 and start as of 1 January for a period of 3 years, with all our out-of-scope staff enjoying the same benefits.

As our company premises winded down for the month-long holiday, I could actually sense the camaraderie of our employees, as I chatted with them from time to time. Everyone had breathed a sigh of relief that no redundancy would be taking place.

One last comment, as an aside pearl of wisdom: it never hurts to have a little fat to spare and the presence of the sword of reason always helps. I will be disclosing our long-term corporate strategy at a more opportune time in the next year.

The Munich plant will be phasing down and close within

the next 2 years. Our operation is the main candidate to take over its higher-value production from this end. So far all looks good for this to materialize when the time comes.

***

CONCLUSION

People management is not easy. Furthermore, people can be highly expensive for any company. An international oil company reckoned that each expatriate employee working abroad and earning about $40,000 a year cost the company a total of $250,000 per year!

This of course, is an extreme example. Yet unless the people-related costs can be closely watched and monitored, it can easily lead to gross salary overpayments, especially at the executive level. It is only a matter of time before this trend is reflected on to gross payroll overpayments throughout the organization.

The global economic crisis is also attributed to have been prompted by too many banks and financial institutions writing too many receivables with little or no collateral as solid assets. The next step, which was that of swapping or trading in these "inflated" receivables naturally aggravated matters even more until the present credit crunch came about.

In the meantime, rates of economic shrinking are alarming high and will hurt businesses that have no access to much-needed liquidity. It could be curbed somewhat if there had been an increase in the volume of lending. However, because the banks have now reverted to their pragmatic and cautious nature, it may be sometime before they can generally start routine lending again to the small businesses regardless of how much governments try to coerce them to do so.

The total global economy will be continue to slow until reduced economic velocity is attained. The message is clear; less spending and lower salaries until better times.

THE END

THE MATCHBOOK ADVERTISING COMPANY

***

JOB DESCRIPTION: Group /Title: JG 10- LEGAL/ PR MANAGER

<u>Scope of Work</u>
The main office and warehouse/shipping works normal a workweek from Monday-Friday between 9.00-18.00 with a one-hour lunch break.

<u>Scope of the Work Coverage</u>
Legal Manager works 9 hours from Monday-Friday and is responsible of all the legal functions in the corporation.

<u>Description of duties</u>:
The Legal/PR Manager leads corporate strategic and tactical legal initiatives and provides senior management with effective advice on company strategies and their implementation, manage the legal function. Legal/ PR Manager will also participate in the definition and development of corporate policies, procedures and provide continuing counsel and guidance on legal and public matters and on legal implications of all matters. Also serve as key legal advisor on all major business transactions, including mergers, acquisitions, and joint ventures and negotiate if necessary.

<u>Mental/Education requirement</u>:
Law degree required (MBA degree is a +)

Skill/Experience required:
5 years or more experience in similar position is required. Strong verbal and written communication skill. Strong level of attention to detail. Must be a good negotiator.

Physical Effort needed:
10% moving about and 90% sitting.

Responsibilities/Impact on results:
Responsible of all the legal and PR functions.

Working Conditions/Safety
The plant is located about 6 kilometers from the center of the town.

Points (x Factor)
5010-5530-6050 (x0.9)

THE MATCHBOOK ADVERTISING COMPANY

***

JOB DESCRIPTION- Job and Title: JG 6- Services Staff

Scope of Work
The factory operates on a production schedule of 2x8-hour shifts, between 0800-2400 hours and the main office and warehouse/shipping works normal a workweek from Monday-Friday between 9.00 -18.00 with a one-hour lunch .

Scope of coverage
Services staff are primarily responsible for coordinating and arranging all the necessary plant and office services.

Description of duties:
Services staff is basically responsible for arranging and coordinating activity for all transportation schedules with contractor for 151 shift workers and 26 office staff. Procurement of foods and meats as well as cleaning materials for the plant. Making travel bookings for all marketing and other staff travel on company business. Keeping all records for medical treatment and Social Insurance formalities and all other matters related to services

Mental/ Education requirement:
Minimum high school graduate with high level of knowledge on the properties of the job he is responsible for.

105

Skill/Experience required:
No experience required. Must be fast and diligent, have the ability to solve problems efficiently and be able and willing to serve.

Physical Effort needed:
80% moving around 20% sitting

Responsibilities/Impact on results:
Must ensure taking care of all necessary services such as transport, cleaning, meals, etc.

Working Conditions
The plant is located about 6 kilometers from the center of the town.

Points (x Factor)
2160-2405-2650 (x1.4)

***

JOB DESCRIPTION-Job Group and Title: JG10 Finance Manager

Scope of Work
The factory operates on a production schedule of 2x8-hour shifts, between 0800-2400 hours and the main office and warehouse/shipping works normal a workweek from Monday-Friday between 9.00-18.00 with a one-hour lunch. The turnover is about $50 million per year.

Scope of Work Coverage
The Finance Manager is responsible for all company financial transactions.

Description of duties:
Prepares and leads consultations for the company annual budget and yearly forecasts, and timely management controls of expenditures. Produces longterm cash flow forecasts to assist in defining company strategies. Produces uptodate accurate monthly finance reports including review of monthly performance. His main brief is cash flow management and establishing sound relationship with the banks regarding funding requirements and sound credit control practices, monitored to ensure minimum debtor days. Produce monthly Balance Sheet reconciliations.

Mental and education requirement:
Must have at least 3 years experience in a similar position. Chartered Accountancy qualification is highly desirable. University graduate, preferably from economics or in

a business science; Masters' degree is an asset. Good command of English is essential.

Skill/Experience required:
Experienced in financial reporting and management information systems. A good level of attention to detail is needed as well as and spreadsheet skills in Microsoft Excel and other Office Packages. Should have good human relation skills, positive attitude and communication skills. Must be able to persuade and negotiate with colleagues.

Physical Effort needed:
5% standing and 15% moving about and 80% sitting.

Responsibilities/Impact on results:
Responsible for all company financial functions. Company plant and inventory is currently estimated at US$ 1 billion.
Working Conditions/Safety
The office is located about 6 kilometers from the center of the town.
Points (x Factor)
5010 – 5530 – 6050 (x 0.9)

***

JOB DESCRIPTION- Job Group and Title: JG5 Electrician

Scope of Work
The factory operates on a production schedule of 2x8-hour shifts, between 0800-2400 hours and the main office and warehouse/shipping works normal a workweek from Monday-Friday between 9.00-18.00 with a one-hour lunch break.

Scope of coverage
The jobholder is primarily responsible for ensuring that all electrical systems in the factory as well as all other areas in the whole premise are functioning properly.
Description of duties:
The electrician periodically inspects the electrical systems in the factory and office buildings (circuits, outlets, load centres, panel boards, etc) and repair motors, transformers, generators, and electronic controllers on machine tools as well as industrial robots and other electrical equipment. Most of the electrician's time is on preventive maintenance by periodically inspecting equipment to locate and correct problems before breakdowns occur and to advise management if continued operation of equipment could be hazardous. If breakdowns occur, the electrician must make the necessary repairs as quickly as possible to minimize inconvenience, replacing circuit breakers, fuses, switches, electrical and electronic components, or wires. He works in close coordination with the maintenance mechanics.

Mental/Education requirement:
The company electrician should be a graduate from a technical crafts school and must be qualified by the state ministerial inspecting organization.

Skill/Experience required:
The jobholder must have at least 5 years experience in a similar environment and must display basic courtesy in human relations.

Physical Effort needed:
50% standing, 10% sitting and 40% moving about.

Responsibilities/Impact on results:
The jobholder is responsible for uninterrupted power supply in the plant. The impact of electrical breakdown on the factory production could be extensive.

Working Conditions/Safety
The plant is located about 6 kilometers from the center of the town.

Points (x Factor
(x1.2) 1760 – 1955 - 2150

***

JOB DESCRIPTION- Job Group/Title: Receptionist/ Tel Operator JG6

Scope of Work
The factory operates on a production schedule of 2x8-hour shifts, between 0800-2400 hours and the main office and warehouse/shipping works normal a workweek from Monday-Friday between 9.00-18.00 with a one-hour lunch break.

Scope of coverage
The jobholder is the first point of contact for all visitors to the company. Jobholder is also responsible for all telephone communications, greets visitors, receives and routes mail, computerized faxes and answers all telephone calls.

Description of duties:
The jobholder answers all telephones, routes documents and letters and performs other clerical tasks around the office. The receptionist also keeps a log of visitors with arrival and departure times. Other duties may include sorting mail, maintaining logs for employee attendance, proofreading outgoing letters, reports, and e-mails, and keeping the reception area generally neat.

Mental/Education requirement:
Minimum high school graduate with previous receptionist experience.

Skill/Experience required:
The jobholder needs to have 2 years experience in a similar environment and display basic courtesy in human relations, with good phone voice, smart, polite with a service-oriented attitude. Must be punctual. Basic Computer Skills such as word and excel an asset.

Physical Effort needed:
30% standing, 50% sitting and 20% moving about. .

Responsibilities/Impact on results:
The jobholder is responsible for a good company image by making a good first impression.

Working Conditions/Safety
The plant is located about 6 kilometers from the center of the town.

Points (x Factor) (x1.2) 2160- 2405- 2650

***

JOB DESCRIPTION- Job Group and Title: JG4 Forklift Operator

Scope of Work
The factory operates on a production schedule of 2x8-hour shifts, between 0800-2400 hours and the main office and warehouse/shipping works normal a workweek from Monday-Friday between 9.00-18.00 with a one-hour lunch break.

Scope of coverage
The Forklift Operator is on duty during normal working hours and is responsible for ensuring that all shipping and storage of product is handled efficiently.

Description of duties:
Operating the forklift using manual pallet jacks as well as performing basic stocking and cleaning duties. Manual handling of some materials (40lbs on average) is needed. Must have had previous shipping and receiving experience.

Mental/Education requirement:
Preferably Crafts/Technical School graduate.

Skill/Experience required:
The Forklift Operator should have worked in a similar warehouse environment and experienced in driving within

narrow areas with sensitive equipment. Keen eyesight essential.

Physical Effort needed:
70% moving about(forklift), 10% sitting and 20% standing

Responsibilities/Impact on results:
The forklift operator is vital in ensuring that products are shipped on time and that they are stored in the warehouse after production. Failure can result in significant production loss.

Working Conditions/Safety
The plant is located about 6 kilometers from the center of the town and nearest fire station. Extreme care for fire hazard is vital.

Points (x Factor)
1430 – 1590 – 1750 (x1.2)

***

JOB DESCRIPTION- Job Group and Title: JG11 Production Manager

Scope of Work
The factory operates on a production schedule of 2x8-hour shifts, between 0800-2400 hours and the main office and warehouse/shipping works normal a workweek from Monday-Friday between 9.00-18.00 with a one-hour lunch break.

Scope of coverage
The Prod Mgr is primarily responsible for overseeing shift operations at the plant and ensuring that proper and effective operation takes place.

Description of duties:
Plans, organizes, schedules, assigns and evaluates the work of all shift plant workers, supervisors and maintenance staff; provides training and counselling, as needed. Assures proper safety standards and precautions are followed; assures that effective safety training is made. Inspects plant processes and equipment, assuring proper working order; reviews plant operation logs and equipment failure reports. Researches and prepares reports related to the work; writes engineering specifications for plant and equipment improvements. Makes sure that shift and work schedules are properly administered. Conducts employee evaluations, responds to complaints and grievances and takes disciplinary actions as needed. Plans maintenance activities for maintenance personnel. Orders parts,

chemicals, and equipment for plant operations, and safety equipment. Prepares annual plant budget.

Mental/Education requirement:

Must be a graduate from an engineering discipline. Intellectual maturity and pleasant personality is essential. Good knowledge of safety standards in plant ops.

Skill/Experience required:

Min 7 years in similar position with ability to plan, organize, schedule, assign, and evaluate the work of plant staff. Needs to be experienced in diagnosis and assessment of operational problems by taking appropriate corrective actions. Effective working relationships with employees and general public

Physical Effort needed:

15% standing, 50% sitting and 35% moving about.

Responsibilities/Impact on results:

The jobholder is responsible overall well-being of all plant staff. The impact of problems could be extensive.

Working Conditions/Safety

The plant is located about 6 kilometers from the center of the town.

Points (x Factor)

(x1.3) 6060- 6755 - 7450

**

JOB DESCRIPTION- Job Group and Title: JG 6- Accounting Staff

Scope of Work
The factory operates on a production schedule of 2x8-hour shifts, between 0800-2400 hours and the main office and warehouse/shipping works normal a workweek from Monday-Friday between 9.00-18.00 with a one-hour lunch break.

Scope of coverage
Accounting staff are primarily responsible for recording of all financial transactions and making company accounting entries.

Description of duties:
Accounting staff are basically responsible for keepings records of all financialtransactions. They enter and keep records of all transactions and calculate tax requirements as needed. They are also responsible for the timely payment of all company salaries and banking formalities for 177 employees.

Mental/Education requirement:
Minimum high school graduate with good level of knowledge of basic accounting procedures.

Skill/Experience required:
Although no experience is required, 1-2 years in similar

job is an advantage. Must be fast and diligent and have the ability to solve problems efficiently with ability and willingness to serve people.

Physical Effort needed:
80% sitting, 20% moving about.   :

Responsibilities/Impact on results
Must ensure proper accounting is recorded.

Working Conditions/Safety :
The plant is located about 6 kilometers from the center of the town.

Points (x Factor)
2160-2405-2650 (x1.2)

***

JOB DESCRIPTION- Job Group and Title: Sales Staff JG 8

<u>Scope of Work</u>
Sales staff may work more than 40 hours per week because of the nature of the work and the amount of travel. The factory operates on a production schedule of 2x8-hour shifts, between 0800-2400 hours and the main office and warehouse/shipping works normal a workweek from Monday-Friday between 9.00-18.00 with a one-hour lunch break.

<u>Scope of coverage</u>
Responsible for all sales activities, from lead generation through close in an assigned territory. Develops and implements agreed upon Marketing Plan which will meet both personal and business goals of expanding customer base in the marketing area. Works with sales and support team in customer satisfaction, revenue generation, and long-term account goals.

<u>Description of duties</u>:
Most of Sales Staff time is on telephone communication and resolving problems or complaints about product. The Sales staff travel extensively for visits with current clients and prospective buyers. They show samples, catalog and describe items of their company stocks, informing customers of prices, availability, and ways in which product can save money and boost productivity. Sales staff may

need to emphasize unique product qualities and address any clients' questions or concerns. Sales staff demonstrate product and explain how use of product can reduce costs and increase sales. They analyze sales statistics; prepare reports; and handle administrative duties, such expense accounts, scheduling appointments, and making travel plans. They are up-to-date on new and existing products and monitor sales, prices, and products of their competitors. Process of promoting and selling the product may take up to several months. Sales Staff often will immediately answer technical and non-technical questions about the products. Recording of interactions with clients for better match their future needs and sales potential.

Mental/Education requirement:
University graduate in business with 2-3 years previous experience. Intellectual maturity a must.

Skill/Experience required:
Attention to detail, organized and results oriented, able to work fast and good with figures.

Physical Effort needed:
40% standing, 10% sitting and 50% moving about.

Responsibilities/Impact on results:
Sales staff must always meet with clients. Failure to do so may have adverse affects.

Working Conditions/Safety
Sales staff may need to travel for several days or weeks at times. Sales staff often stand for long periods and may need to carry heavy sample products, necessitating some

physical stamina. Sales staff may work more than 40 hours
per week because of the need for travel.

Points (x Factor)

3310 – 3655 – 4000 (x 1.2)

***

JOB DESCRIPTION- Job Group/Title:JG 1- SHIFT WORKER

Scope of Work
On each 2 8-hour shifts, there are 4 belts with
10 shift workers each for 2000 irons per day
2 belts with 8 shift workers each for 1000 Water Fountains
per day
8 belts with 10 shift workers each for 2000 hair conditioners
per day

Scope of the Shift Worker Coverage
Incumbent is a shift worker on prod belt

Description of duties:
Shift Worker is one of 8-10 workers who perform basically
REPETITIVE and BORING work for the safe and
uninterrupted production of unique household appliances.
The production belt will suspend activity for 30- minutes
in mid shifts to allow for a meal break as coordinated and
monitored by the shift Foreman.

Mental/Education requirement:
Must be able to change wiring in any simple electric
wall plug. Minimum primary school graduate with some
knowledge of technical basics.

Skill/Experience required:
No previous experience required. Must display basic

politeness in human relations and should undergo 2-week basic factory training, including safety. Danger of the work requires immediate preventive reaction for protection to factory and to self.

<u>Physical Effort needed</u>:
85% standing and 15% moving about. Must be able and robust.

<u>Responsibilities/Impact on results</u>:
Could be partly responsible for $45000 worth of product during each shift and could be eventually responsible for worst-case production loss of $630000 per week.

<u>Working Conditions/Safety</u>
High noise, rapidly moving machine parts and presence of safety hazards

<u>Points (x Factor)</u>
760 -   845 -   930 (x1)

***

JOB DESCRIPTION-Job Group/Title: JG12 PLANT MGR

Scope of Work

The factory operates a production schedule of 2x8-hour shifts, between 0800-2400 hours. The main office and warehouse/shipping works normal a workweek from Monday-Friday between 9.00-18.00 with one-hour lunch break.

Scope of Coverage

Plant Manager is the senior employee and delegate for General Manager. He is on call 24 hours a day in addition to regular office hours during weekdays.

Description of duties:

Direct and coordinate plant operations within company policies and procedures. Maintain a clean and safe plant. Establish and direct plant polices and procedures. Responsible for plant production goals. Establish and maintain a positive community relationship. Foster a well-trained and motivated staff. Confer with department heads to ensure coordination of purchasing, production, and shipping. Conduct employee performance reviews. Schedule and conduct plant meetings. Select and train plant supervisory and administrative staff and approve shift production schedules. Schedule corporate and plant meetings as delegate for the Gen. Mgr.

Mental/Education requirement:

Should preferably be a University graduate from an engineering discipline or business. MBA is a +

Skill/Experience required:
Direction of plant operations and community relations requires significant manufacturing knowledge as well as advanced interpersonal and supervisory skills. This is normally acquired by at least seven to ten years of manufacturing experience, which would include supervisory responsibility.

Physical Effort needed:
30% standing and 25% moving about and 45% sitting. Must be able and robust.

Working Conditions/Safety
The plant is located about 6 kilometers from the center of the town.(located in the same premise as the plant) The GM is ultimately responsible for the whole company plant and inventory, which is currently estimated at US$ 1 billion.

Points (x Factor)
7460- 8305 – 9150 (x1.6)

***

JOB DESCRIPTION-Job Group and Title: Secretary, JG 7 and Exec Secrt. JG8

Scope of Work
The factory operates on a production schedule of 2x7-hour shifts, between 0800-2400 hours and the main office and warehouse/shipping works normal a workweek from Monday-Friday between 9.00-13.00 with a one-hour lunch break.

Scope of Work Coverage
The jobholder is primarily responsible for producing business documents and to provide secret arial services to the company managers.

Description of duties:
The jobholder is required to prepare all routine and other documents, including but not limited to recording of minutes in all executive and other business meetings. The Secretary contributes in the preparation of annual reports other official files. The secretary's basic functions include all routine general office functions such as answering telephone call and inquiries in a knowledge able and professional manner.

Mental and education requirement:
Secretary must have ability to communicate, meet and deal tactfully with the public and co-workers and must be willing to overlap with co-workers' job descriptions whenever required.

Skill/Experience required:

The jobholder needs to have at least two years related experience and must display basic courtesy in human relations. He/She must have equivalent combination of education and experience as well as courses in secretarial work and office administration is a +.

Physical Effort needed:

40% standing and 20% moving about and 40% sitting.

Responsibilities/Impact on results:

The jobholder is responsible for attending all management meetings, recording and preparing minutes of business meetings for distribution to managers. Other work includes mailing, photocopying and other office functions.

Working Conditions/Safety

The plant is located about 6 kilometers from the center of the town.

JG 7 (x factor) 2660-2980-3300 (x0.9) JG 8 (x factor) 3310- 3655 – 4000 (x 1.2)

***

JOB DESCRIPTION-Job Group/Title: JG6 Pack/ Shipping Staff

Scope of Work
The factory operates on a production schedule of 2x8-hour shifts, between 0800-2400 hours and the main office and warehouse/shipping works normal a workweek from Monday-Friday between 9.00-18.00 with one-hour lunch break.

Scope of coverage
The jobholder is primarily responsible for packing, loading/unloading finished product and raw materials stock and to maintain warehouse inventory.

Description of duties
Package finished product for shipping (shrink wrapping, boxing, labeling). Stage finished product for loading. Load finished product onto truck and/or railcar. Unload raw materials from truck, aircraft, and/or railcar. Move raw materials to warehouse storage. Move waste from assembly line to dumper trucks. Responsible for quality control. No damaged product is sent out. No damaged raw material is accepted in. Operate within standard operating procedures and Job Safety Analysis Operate forklift, trucks, and/or railcars. Complete daily logs. Perform preventive maintenance on forklift, truck, and/ or railcar. Communicate with operators from other shifts. Clean and maintain work area. Turn off and lock out equipment when not in use.

Mental/Education requirement:
Basic reading, writing, and arithmetic skills. This is normally acquired through a high school diploma or equivalent. Forklift certification and applicable state certification for truck and/or rail operation required

Skill/Experience required:
The jobholder must have at least 3 years experience in a similar environment and must display basic courtesy in human relations and Manual dexterity required for operating machinery. Ability to lift up to 50 kgs required

Physical Effort needed:
10% standing, 40% sitting, 50% moving about.

Responsibilities/Impact on results:
The jobholder is responsible for ensuring proper packing and shipment of inspected product. Impact of failure and shipment of defective product will have severe impact on company image and quality certification.

Working Conditions/Safety
The plant is located about 6 kilometers from the center of the town. Work involves frequent lifting of materials and product up to 50 kgs. Machinery operation requires the use of safety equipment to include but not limited to; eye safety glasses, hearing protectors, work boots, and hardhats. Loose fitting clothes and jewelry are not permitted.

Points (x Factor)
(x1.2) 2160-   2405 2650

***

JOB DESCRIPTION-Job Group& Title: JG5 Maint. Mechanic

Scope of Work
The factory operates on a production schedule of 2x8-hour shifts, between 0800-2400 hours and the main office and warehouse/shipping works normal a workweek from Monday-Friday between 9.00-18.00 with a one-hour lunch break.

Scope of coverage
The jobholder is primarily responsible for the maintenance and repair of plant production machinery.

Description of duties:
The jobholder monitors all machinery for possible damages. The mechanic also repairs machines or mechanical devices whenever operators or supervisors request this service. Immediate action is needed to avoid interruption of workflow.

Mental/Education requirement:
Must have maintenance experience in similar industry or factory. Minimum primary school graduate with some knowledge of technical basics.
Skill/Experience required:
The jobholder must have at least 1 years experience in a similar environment and must display basic courtesy in human relations and has to be careful, skilled and self-disciplined .

Physical Effort needed:
50% standing, 10% sitting and 40% moving about.

Responsibilities/Impact on results:
The jobholder is responsible for proper operation of all plant machinery.

Working Conditions/Safety
The plant is located about 6 kilometers from the center of the town.

Points (x Factor)
1760   1955   2150   x1.2

***

JOB DESCRIPTION-Job Group and Title: JG 4 Amb. Driver/Nurse

Scope of Work
The factory operates on a production schedule of 2x8-hour shifts, between 0800-2400 hours and the main office and warehouse/shipping works normal a workweek from Monday-Friday between 9.00-18.00 with a one-hour lunch break.

Scope of coverage
The jobholder is primarily responsible for driving the ambulance and maintenance of the vehicle/equipment. Daily vehicle inspection and equipment checklist.

Description of duties:
The jobholder drives ambulance to transport sick, injured, convalescent persons with patients on stretcher. Takes sick or injured persons to hospital, or convalescents to destination, using knowledge and skill in driving to avoid sudden motions detrimental to patients. Changes soiled linen on stretcher. Administers first aid as needed. May need to suppress violent patients and report facts concerning accident or emergency to hospital personnel or law enforcement officials.

Mental/Education requirement:
Current/valid drivers license. First Aid training. Must complete passenger sensitivity training.

Skill/Experience required:
3 years previous experience required. The Jobholder must have a caring attitude, have excellent communication and interpersonal skills and make fast decisions, be physically fit and emotionally resilient to stay calm under pressure.

Physical Effort needed:
20 % standing, 50% sitting and 30% moving about. Must possess physical agility necessary to assist ambulatory, wheelchair bound, and others with disabilities to safely board/exit transit vehicles.

Responsibilities/Impact on results:
The jobholder is responsible for well-being of patients and to ensure that patients are properly delivered for urgent medical treatment. He may have life and death responsibility over people and needs serious attention to detail.

Working Conditions/Safety
The plant is located about 6 kilometers from the center of the town.

Points (x 1.2 Factor)
1430   1590   1750

***

JOB DESCRIPTION-Job Group and Title: JG 1-CLEANER

Scope of Work
The factory operates on a production schedule of 2x8-hour shifts, between 0800-2400 hours. The main office and warehouse/shipping works normal a workweek from Monday-Friday between 9.00-18.00 with one-hour lunch break. The whole plant, warehouse and office area must be cleaned to increase productivity of the workers and provide a healthy and clean work environment for workers.

Scope of coverage
The cleaners work on a 12-hour rotation schedule.

Description of duties:
The cleaner is one of 6 people who follow a preset plan for vacuuming all manufacturing areas and corridors, empty waste bins, sweep and mops floor surfaces, clean all toilets and other areas as assigned. The cleaners also report anything needing repair or replacement to the appropriate person and are required to maintain polite and good communication with all colleagues and company staff.

Mental/Education requirement:
Incumbents need to have primary school education with some knowledge of basics of good hygiene.

Skill/Experience required:

Basically, no experience is needed but they must display basic politeness in human relations and need to undergo 2-day orientation training, including fire prevention and safety, as they may be required to react immediately in emergency to protect the factory and its staff.

Physical Effort needed:
60% standing and 40% moving about. .

Responsibilities/Impact on results:
Minimal.

Working Conditions/Safety
The plant is located about 6 kilometers from the center of the town.

Points (x Factor)
760 -   845 -   930 (x1)

***

JOB DESCRIPTION-Job Group and Title: JG 3-SECURITY GUARD

<u>Scope of Work</u>
The factory operates on a production schedule of 2x8-hour shifts, between 0800-2400 hours. The main office and warehouse/shipping works a normal workweek from Monday-Friday between 9.00-18.00 with one-hour lunch break. The whole plant, warehouse and office area must be protected against theft and other hazards.

<u>Scope of Coverage</u>
Security guard works on a 12-hour rotation schedule.

<u>Description of duties</u>:
Security guard is one of 7 people who follow a strict control routine and rounds of the ground. During work hours, incumbent is responsible for escorting visitors. They check all entry and exit to the factory premises as well as all workers arriving and departing the area. They are the first-point contact in the event of emergency, including fire breakouts or unauthorized entries. They make recommendations to management in areas where possible breach of security is foreseen.

<u>Mental/Education requirement</u>:
Incumbents should have completed high school with knowledge of first aid and/or combat basics.

Skill/Experience required:
2-3 years experience in similar position is required. They must display basic politeness in human relations and undergo 2-week basic orientation training, including that of fire prevention and safety. They are required to react immediately to protect the factory and its staff.

Physical Effort needed:
30% standing and 25% moving about and 45% sitting. Must be able and robust.

Responsibilities/Impact on results:
At any one time incumbent could be responsible for $ 75 million of product at the warehouse.

Working Conditions/Safety
The plant is located about 6 kilometers from the center of the town.

Points (x Factor)   1160 – 1290 - 1420 (x1)

***

JOB DESCRIPTION-Job Group and Title: JG 4-SHIFT QUALITY CONTROL FOREMAN

Scope of Work
On each 2 8-hour shifts, there are
4 belts with 10 shift workers each for 2000 irons per day
2 belts with 8 shift workers each for 1000 Water Fountains per day
8 belts with 10 shift workers each for 2000 Hair Conditioners per day.

Scope of Coverage
Incumbent is one of 3 foremen on duty for each production belt

Description of duties:
Shift Foreman is one of 3 foremen responsible for ensuring quality control and safe, uninterrupted flow of production on the production line. Foreman must rotate workers to allow for break of 10 minutes each for each one hour of work. Foreman will also cover for any incapacitated worker and/or can stop production at any time.

Mental/Education requirement:
Must know basics of mechanics and electricity and able to read and apply blueprints and project plans. Graduate or minimum last year student at Technical Crafts School.

Skill/Experience required:

2-3 years in similar manufacturing plant position and capable in human relations. Should have undergone 2-week basic factory training. Danger of the work requires immediate reaction to prevent bodily harm to shift workers.

Physical Effort needed:
75% standing and 25% moving about. Must be able and robust.

Responsibilities/Impact on results:
Partly responsible for $ 45,000 production during each shift. If foreman does not react on time, he could be responsible for worst-case production loss of $ 630,000 per week.

Working Conditions/Safety
High noise, rapidly moving machine parts and presence of safety hazards

Points (x Factor)
1430 -   1590 - 1750 (x1.2)

***

JOB DESCRIPTION-Job Group and Title: JG 2-COOK

Scope of Work
The factory operates on a production schedule of 2x8-hour shifts, between 0800-2400 hours and the main office and warehouse/shipping works normal a workweek from Monday-Friday between 9.00-18.00 with a one-hour lunch break. The cook is required to prepare lunch for 70-80 people and to maintain a clean and sterile kitchen with hygienic environment.

Scope of coverage
The cook is primarily responsible for preparing a tasty, balanced and healthy meal served under sanitary conditions at the company-dining hall.

Description of duties:
The cook is responsible for personally buying meats, vegetables and other supplies within budget and to cook a menu as instructed by the Services Staff responsible for office administration and services. The cook is assisted by one helper/cleaner in preparing and serving of the lunch (self-service) and to supervise washing of dishes and cutlery after the meal as well as casseroles, pots and pans and kitchen equipment such as freezers and ovens. The cook is also responsible for supervising helper in serving tea and coffee in the office.

<u>Mental/Education requirement</u>:
The cook needs to have a primary school education with some knowledge of dietary basics.

<u>Skill/Experience required</u>:
The cook needs at least 5 years experience in a similar environment and display basic politeness in human relations and persuasive in pleasing people with his/her meals. He/she must be robust and able because of job needs. The cook must undergo a 2-day orientation training, including fire prevention and safety as he/she may be required to react immediately in emergency.

<u>Physical Effort needed</u>:
80% standing, 7% sitting and 13% moving about. .

<u>Responsibilities/Impact on results</u>:
Must ensure a balanced diet for all staff.

<u>Working Conditions/Safety</u>
The plant is located about 6 kilometers from the center of the town.

<u>Points (x Factor)</u>
940 -   1045 - 1150 (x1)

***

JOB DESCRIPTION-Job Group/title: GENERAL MANAGER, JG 13

<u>Scope of Work</u>
The main office and warehouse -shipping works a normal workweek from Monday-Friday between 9.00-18.00 with a one-hour lunch. The production plant operates 11 months in the year on 2x8hour shifts.

<u>Scope of Work Coverage</u>
SOFI Corporation produces unique electrical household appliances and is located in Bozüyük (Turkey). The General Manager has overall manufacturing and marketing responsibility for this fully integrated company employing nearly 200 direct company employees and contractors providing different services.

<u>Description of duties</u>:
The General Manager of the company is mainly responsible for profitability and stock value of the company through accurate strategic planning. The General Manager reports directly to the board of directors at the group main office in Geneva and is ultimately responsible for profitability and management of the plant. Executive action takes place by delegation to the department managers.

<u>Mental and education requirement</u>:
A degree in an engineering discipline is desirable; an MBA degree is a plus.

Skill/Experience required:
A minimum of 10-year experience is required at an international position in a similar industry. Fluency in English (and one other European or Asian language) is essential. He needs to possess a high level of intellectual maturity to properly manage this challenging job.

Physical Effort needed:
10% standing and 30% moving about and 60% sitting.

Responsibilities/Impact on results:
The General Manager is not only responsible for his own actions but also for that of others in the company. He is vested with full responsibility in all executive action and financial action, either directly or by others in the company. Most of his activity is interaction with employees and major clients. The overall value of the company shares on the stock market is directly related to his industrial action.

Working Conditions/Safety
The office is located about 6 kilometers from the center of the town.

Points (x Factor)
9170-   10210 - 11250 (x 1.9)

***

JOB DESCRIPTION_(Job Group and Title: JG 11 – Marketing Manager)

Scope of Work

Sofi Corporation produces household and small electrical appliances is a manufacturer located In Bozüyük, Bilecik. The management and operations work a 5 day normal week, 9 hours daily between 9:00 to 18:00, with a 1 hour lunch break. The MM is responsible for sales in excess of YTL 74 million per annum. He logs an average of 2 days travel every month.

Scope of Coverage

Responsible for developing and maintaining marketing strategies to meet organizational objectives. He manages the application of marketing strategies and techniques and the management of the firm's marketing resources.

Description of duties:

The Marketing Manager is responsible to establish and develop distribution networks for the company product lines. He ensures that quality services are provided to all customers by company marketing staff. Initiates market research studies or surveys and is responsible for analyzing and advising R&D toward new and better products, packaging and delivery of products. Directs and evaluates ongoing marketing strategies, which allow for sales departments to provide better and more saleable products. To manage the Marketing Department Budget.

Mental/Education requirement:
The MM must possess good communication skills and diplomacy, skill in statistics and trend analysis, be a good decision maker with negotiating and persuasive skills, have professional level Microsoft Office skills, minimum Marketing or Business Administration major graduate, preferably have an MBA degree.

Skill/Experience required:
Minimum 5 years of sales experience in marketing in a similar industry. Experience with enterprise with software solutions in large, complex organizations is preferable. Extensive experience in all aspects of developing and maintaining marketing strategies to meet organizational objectives. Strong understanding of customer and market dynamics and requirements. Willingness to travel and work in a global team of professionals. Must be fluent in English. Another European or Asian language is preferable.

Physical Effort needed:
20% standing, 70% sitting and 10% moving about. Ability to travel all around the world with good car driving skill.

Working Conditions:
The plant is located about 6 kilometers from the center of the town.

Points (x Factor)
6060-6755 – 7450 (x 1.3)

***

Job Group and Title: JG 8- COMPANY DOCTOR (CONSULTANT BASIS)

Scope of Work
The factory operates on a production schedule of 2x8-hour shifts, between 08:00-24:00 hours. The main office and warehouse/shipping works a normal workweek from Monday-Friday between 9.00-18.00, with one-hour lunch break. The company employs 177 people.

Scope of the job
The Company doctor is responsible for general medical care of SOFI employees. The doctor has his own practice in the town center and company employees may visit him as needed.

Description of duties:
The doctor is available at the plant dispensary premises on afternoons 3 times a week for 2 hours each. He or she provides direct patient care in the clinic including assessment, screening, diagnosis,and treatment of patients; He determines the degree of disabilities of the patients and provides medical consultation in his specialization area. He authorizes clearnace for employment from a medical aspect. He is first point in event of accident injuries and will oversee formalities as required until pateient has been admitted to hospital. He also periodically checks hygiene of company meals and environment. Perform other tasks as required.

THE MATCHBOOK ADVERTISING COMPANY

<u>Mental/Education requirement</u>:
Specialization in internal medicine preferred. He must be up to date with terminology, research methods, techniques, and/or sources of information, principles, theories, and practices of medicine and sources of community resources and services.

<u>Skill/Experience required</u>:
Five years experience in similar position is preferred with good diagnostic capability and ability to speak clearly, concisely and effectively. As a company doctor and direct contact with all levels of employees, the major contribution is a caring and humane atitude.

<u>Physical Effort needed</u>:
30% standing, 30% moving about and 40% sitting.

<u>Responsibilities/Impact on results</u>:
The doctor is responsible for all company hygiene in the premises. He must approve the health condition of all employees prior to employment.

<u>Working Conditions/Safety</u>
The plant is located about 5 km from the center of the town.

<u>Salary</u>   3000 YTL

***

JOB DESCRIPTION-Job Group and Title: JG9 Safety Engineer

Scope of Work
The factory operates on a production schedule of 2x8-hour shifts, between 0800-2400 hours and the main office and warehouse/shipping works normal a workweek from Monday-Friday between 9.00-18.00 with a one-hour lunch break. The Safety Engineer is present during production shifts.

Scope of coverage
The Safety Engineer is responsible for planning, organizing, and controlling the safety function to maintain the highest industrial safety standards so that accident-free production can take place in the plant as well as during warehouse and shipping operations. The Engineer is also responsible for taking all measures for total fire control at the worksite in accord with corporate, OSHA, and related safety policies and directives.

Description of duties:
The Safety Engineer is responsible for periodic inspections of plant machinery, equipment, and working conditions to ensure conformance to appropriate safety and sanitary standards and regulations. The Safety Engineer advises on work practices to ensure that protective devices and safe work procedures are used and on a regular basis monitors availability and condition of appropriate fire-fighting

and safety equipment in the plant. He is focal point for contact with local fire department. The Safety Engineer is focal point for liaison with government agencies in case of inquiries and inspections to correct deficiencies and to minimize citations and fines for noncompliance.

Mental/Education requirement:
Bachelor's degree in an engineering discipline with appropriate intellectual maturity.

Skill/Experience required:
The jobholder must have at least 5 years experience in a similar environment and display basic courtesy in human relations.

Physical Effort needed:
50 %standing, 30 %sitting, 20% moving about.

Responsibilities/Impact on results:
The jobholder is responsible for the totality of industrial safety and fire prevention. Total plant assets are in excess of US$1 billion.

Working Conditions/Safety
The plant is located about 6 kilometers from the center of the town and nearest fire station. Extreme care for fire hazard is vital.

Points (x Factor)
4010-4505-5000 (x1.3)

***

JOB DESCRIPTION-Job Group and Title: JG10 Personnel Director

Scope of Work

The factory operates on a production schedule of 2x8-hour shifts, between 0800-2400 hours and the main office and warehouse/shipping works normal a workweek from Monday-Friday between 9.00-18.00 with a one-hour lunch break.

Scope of coverage

The jobholder is primarily responsible for all staffing, employee relations and for industrial relations with labor union to negotiate collective labor contracts.

Description of duties:

The job holder is responsible for keeping sound records of all company employees, recruitment and selection of employees, monitoring working conditions, coordination of employee training, conduct of performance appraisal, effecting employee promotions and transfers, handling of employee service terminations, ensuring that health and safety requirements are met and overall responsibility for employee welfare. He is first point of contact as delegated by the General Manager.

Mental/Education requirement:

A degree in economics or business is preferred with an

MBA a +. Needs to be fluent in English. Must have intellectual maturity and a humane and caring nature.

Skill/Experience required:
The jobholder must have at least 7 years experience in a similar environment and must display basic courtesy in human relations.

Physical Effort needed:
10 % standing, 20% moving about and 7o% sitting.

Responsibilities/Impact on results:
The jobholder is responsible for ensuring that the company enjoys a positive industrial relation image and that best employee relations practice takes place.

Working Conditions/Safety
The plant is located about 6 kilometers from the center of the town.

Points (x Factor)
(x) 5010 - 5530 – 6050 (x 0.9)

FURTHER READING

- **Theory R Management**; Thomas Nelson (September, 1994) Wayne T. Alderson, Nancy Alderson McDonnell, and Nancy Jean Alderson
- **The Conflict Management Skills Workshop: A Trainer's Guide (The Trainer's Workshop(TM) Series)**, AMACOM (February, 2002), Bill Withers.
- **Transforming Work: The Five Keys to Achieving Trust, Commitment, & Passion in the Workplace**, Perseus Publishing (15 December, 2001), Patricia E. Boverie, and Michael Kroth,
- **Your Rights in the Workplace, 4th Ed**, Nolo Press (June, 1999); Barbara Kate Repa and Marcia Stewart.
- **Contented Cows Give Better Milk: The Plain Truth About Employee Relations & Your Bottom Line**; Williford Communications (March, 1998); Bill Catlette and Richard Hadden
- **Do It My Way or You're Fired! Employee Rights and the Changing Role of Management Prerogatives**, John Wiley & Sons (January, 1983), David W. Ewing
- **How to Become a Certified Employee Friendly Workplace: The Pocket Guide to Achieving Excellence in Employee Relations**, InSync Communications (September, 2000), John Wes Spence.
- **Inspiring Commitment: How to Win Employee**

Loyalty in Chaotic Times, McGraw-Hill Trade (01 November, 1995), Anthony Mendes.

- **Kaizen Teian 2: Guiding Continuous Improvement Through Employee Suggestions,** Productivity Press (September, 1997), Japan Human Relations Association

- **The Loyalty Link: How Loyal Employees Create Loyal Customers,** John Wiley & Sons (11 April, 1997), Dennis G. McCarthy.

- **Rights at Work: Employment Relations in the Post-Union Era(A Twentieth Century Fund Book),** The Brookings Institution(May, 1993), Richard Edwards

- **Looking Forward to Monday Morning;** Threshold Group; (01 November, 2001), Diane Hodges

- **Work Naked: Eight Essential Principles for Peak Performance in the Virtual Workplace,** Jossey-Bass (15 May, 2001), Cynthia C. Froggatt.

- **Everyone a Leader: A Grassroots Model for the New Workplace,** John Wiley & Sons (May, 1999), Bergman, Kathleen Hurson, and Darlene Russ-Eft